PLAYING THE GUITAR
THIRD EDITION

By the same author:

First Book for the Guitar

The Guitar Songbook

Solo Guitar Playing

The Renaissance Guitar

The Baroque Guitar

The Classical Guitar

PLAYING THE GUITAR
THIRD EDITION

A Self-Instruction Guide to
Technique and Theory

By Frederick M. Noad, M.A.

SCHIRMER BOOKS
A Division of Macmillan Publishing Co., Inc.
NEW YORK

Collier Macmillan Publishers
LONDON

Schirmer Books
A Division of Macmillan Publishing Co., Inc.
866 Third Avenue, New York, N.Y. 10022

Collier Macmillan Canada, Ltd.

Printed in the United States of America

printing number

11

Library of Congress Cataloging in Publication Data

Noad, Frederick M.
  Playing the guitar.

   1. Guitar—Methods—Self-instruction.
I. Title.
MT588.N59   1981   787.6'1'0712   80-5494
ISBN 0-02-871990-5   AACR2

CONTENTS

Contents

Contents

Contents

PREFACE

This book has been written for the "amateur," in the original sense of "lover" of an instrument. For this reason the reader will not find himself constantly exhorted, as in some methods, to practice for "at least five hours a day"; rather, he is invited to enjoy himself by learning an instrument that is, if more difficult than most people realize, always entertaining.

It is often said that the different styles of guitar playing cannot be mixed, and indeed some teachers discourage their pupils from experiments away from, for instance, the strictly classical field. While agreeing that the professional rarely has time for more than his specialty, I feel that the amateur need not be limited by this esoteric approach. For this reason, I have tried to introduce him to song accompaniment, solo playing, and even flamenco, in the hope of whetting his appetite in the field that most appeals to him while giving a general grounding in technique.

The pieces that I have included have been designed for enjoyment as well as instruction. I know of many guitar methods where the studies serve their precise didactic purpose better, but too often the student is so bored with the result when a piece has been learned that he becomes discouraged and may even give up the instrument. The situation is different when a teacher is present to maintain enthusiasm; but a self-teaching method must speak for itself. My hope is that the readers of this book will derive entertainment and enjoyment from it as well as instruction.

PLAYING THE GUITAR
THIRD EDITION

ABOUT THE GUITAR

The History of the Guitar

The instrument you have chosen to study is one of the oldest known to man. In one form or another it is mentioned as being popular in ancient times in Persia, in many other Middle Eastern countries, and in Rome; and, whether introduced by Romans or Moors, it became the major feature of musical life in Spain. Its forms were as various as were its names, but essentially it was the same instrument that today in its developed form is achieving a popularity and recognition unequaled in the past.

In Europe the guitar was from time to time adopted by the aristocratic world as a fashionable instrument, and several crowned heads studied and played the guitar with the same interest that Queen Elizabeth I gave to the lute. But the credit for the real progress and development of the instrument lies on the one hand with a handful of virtuoso players who placed the guitar in the concert and recital hall, and on the other with the ordinary people who adopted it as a convenient and lively accompaniment to their folk music.

Although most of the great players were Spanish or Italian, they were received with great enthusiasm in other countries, where they often inspired or revived a tremendous local interest. A good example is afforded by the life of Fernando Sor, one of the greatest performers of the past. Trained musically in the famous Montserrat monastery, Sor developed a considerable technique on the guitar and wrote prolifically for it as well as other instruments. In 1813 he went to Paris, where he achieved great recognition and popularity. Later he traveled to London, under the patronage of the Duke of Sussex; there too his performances made the guitar the vogue. From England he went to Prussia and Russia where he was warmly received in St. Petersburg, at that time one of the great musical capitals; he even composed a march for the funeral of Nicholas I. From there he returned to Paris, where he remained until his death in 1839, leaving behind him a wealth of guitar music of a high standard and a number of studies and didactic works also distinguished by their musical value.

After Sor, perhaps the greatest contribution to the growth of the guitar was that of Francisco Tárrega (1852-1909). Although his start in life was constantly hampered by poverty, Tárrega's exceptionally beautiful playing led him to achieve an outstanding success at the Alhambra Theater in Madrid, following which he went to Valencia and Lyons and thence to Paris. His playing there was received with the greatst possible acclaim, an eminent critic noting that he seemed to combine in his instrument the qualities of the violin, piano, and voice as achieved by the most distinguished performers in each of these fields. Certainly all who heard Tárrega said that he produced a completely individual and remarkable beauty of tone from his guitar. After repeating his success in London, Brussels, Berne, and Rome, Tárrega returned to his homeland, where he devoted himself to teaching and composition. This phase marks perhaps his greatest contribution, since his pupils achieved such distinction as soloists and teachers that many consider him the founder of the modern school of guitar technique.

Today it is impossible to think of the concert guitar without associating with it the name of Andrés Segovia, whose performances throughout the world have added immeasurably to the "missionary work" of the previous great soloists. After a distinguished early career, Segovia made his Paris debut in 1924; this brilliant performance, heard by many leading musical figures, was soon followed by an increasing international reputation. Throughout a long and immensely successful career Segovia has worked untiringly for the recognition of the guitar as an instrument for performing both solo and with an orchestra, and has constantly invited and encouraged compositions to increase its literature. All over the world guitar makers, teachers, and students have profited from his freely given advice and encouragement; and in many cities his eagerly awaited concerts have become an annual event of musical enjoyment for the listener and inspiration for the player.

Largely because of the work of Segovia, the modern scene shows an increasing number of excellent players—with more time in the concert hall given to the guitar than ever before—as well as a great increase in the number of teachers and schools of music that now include the guitar in the curriculum.

As an accompaniment to the voice the guitar has historically been almost ideal; it is portable as well as harmonically complete and tonally a good contrast. In a sense the modern folk and popular singer–guitarists are descendants of the medieval troubadours, whose noble tradition of free form has left much room for creative work by the individual in his expression of folk tradition. The music of almost all nations exists on two levels: the compositions of its composers for the polished world of the concert hall; and the creations of the people, passed from father to son, which grow and change with the passage of time as they sing from sheer joy of expression or to relieve and escape from their sorrows and poverty or to retell the stories of their heritage. Folk music—as the music of the people is usually termed—expresses in its lyrics a wisdom and beauty derived from the ordinary events of human life; its music is rich with spontaneity and melodies that have borne the test of time. Both groups borrow from each other, the composer finding a fertile source in vigorous themes of unknown origin, and the people from time to time adopting and absorbing into their tradition a melody or song of a composer.

In Spain, particularly, the guitar was adopted by the people, and from its use to accompany the songs of Andalusia arose the very rich and musically interesting tradition of the flamenco guitar.

The American settlers took along their songs and dances, some of which have been preserved here while forgotten in their country of origin. In addition, the songs of the new country developed further as pioneers, soldiers, cowboys, and miners added their contributions; and side by side with these came the development of the music of the Afro-American, whose spirituals, work songs, and later "blues" have added so much to the American heritage of folk music. In all these types of songs the guitar has been important as the favorite and most widely used instrument of accompaniment; together with the new music new rhythms and styles have evolved for the guitar.

Although the guitar has been adapted structurally for specific uses, the Spanish six-string guitar—the most expressive and adaptable of all types—is the most advanced in both its construction and its technique. Whether you wish to play a concerto, experiment with the intricacies of modern harmony, or just play a simple song, this is your instrument. The story of the Spanish guitar is by no means ended, nor are its possibilities yet fully explored.

Buying a Guitar

The purchase of a first instrument often presents a problem to the beginner, who has no experience to guide him and whose untrained ear is of little assistance. Unfortunately, some of the most enthusiastic salesmen know even less, and thus a considerable sum is often spent on something totally unsuitable. If possible, it is always best to obtain the assistance of a good player or teacher. In any case, the following section should be read carefully as a guide to what to look for and what to avoid. Figure 1 shows the guitar in detail; the names of the parts should be carefully noted so that the text may be fully understood.

The best guitars, like violins, are made not by factories but by individual craftsmen, who make their instruments by hand from the finest woods available. These craftsmen have usually undergone a long and painstaking apprenticeship with an established master craftsman, from whom they have learned the fine points of woodworking and the traditions and secrets of this branch of it. They achieve success when their instruments are chosen by good players for use in the concert hall; and although their instruments are more expensive than mass-produced ones, their profits are usually small in view of the high cost of good materials and the length of time involved in this painstaking hand labor. It is fortunate for the player that such dedicated craftsmen still exist; the purchase of one of their instruments is usually a rewarding investment.

It is impossible to mention all such makers, and invidious to distinguish between the great ones, since above a certain standard the choice depends largely on purely personal preference. Spain has many makers, often with a family tradition of guitar construction, as exemplified by the Ramirez and Esteso families of Madrid. The name of Santos Hernandez became legendary, and fine guitars of similar dimensions in the Hernandez style were produced in Madrid by Marcelo Barbero, Manuel Ramirez, and Domingo Esteso, and in Andalusia by Miguel Rodriguez of Cordoba. Later makers in the Hernandez style include Manuel de la Chica of Granada and Aguado y Hernandez of Madrid. Slightly larger in some dimensions and also of excellent quality are the guitars of José Ramirez of Madrid and the late Ignacio Fleta of Barcelona. Tending in the other direction, José Romanillos—now in England—has produced some smaller guitars of

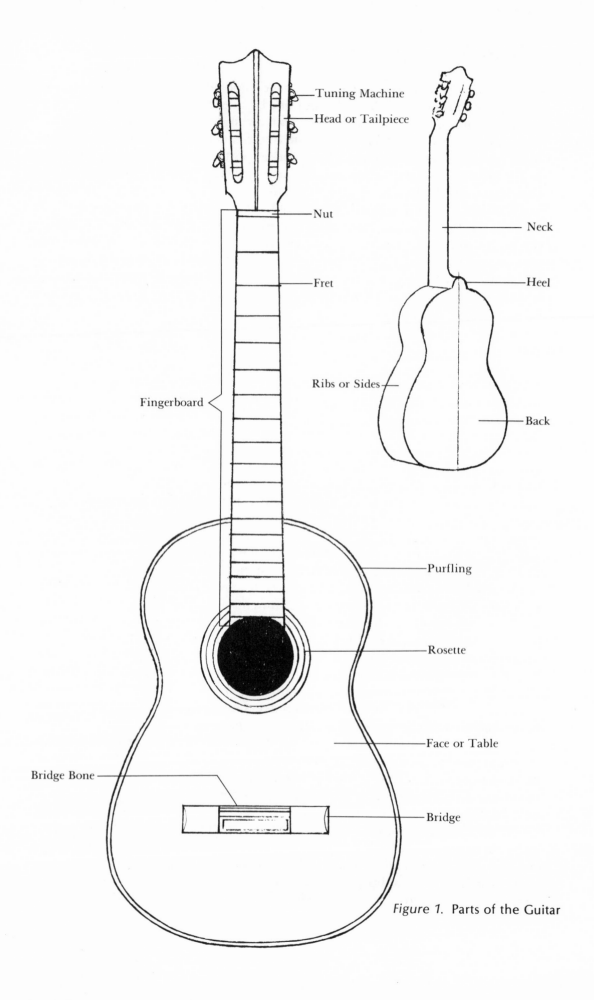

Tuning Machine

Head or Tailpiece

Nut

Neck

Fret

Heel

Fingerboard

Ribs or Sides

Back

Purfling

Rosette

Face or Table

Bridge Bone

Bridge

Figure 1. Parts of the Guitar

surprising volume and beauty of tone. For his marvelous flamenco guitars Arc-ángel Fernandez, a former apprentice of Barbero, is perhaps the most respected maker in Spain today.

In other countries individual makers have achieved distinction, although mainly by following Spanish construction traditions. Perhaps the most famous was Hermann Hauser of Germany, who made an instrument of amazing quality for Andrés Segovia. Worldwide reputations are enjoyed by Kono of Japan, David Rubio of England, José Oribe of the United States, and many others.

In spite of the foregoing, it is a mistake to buy a guitar by name alone. Unfortunately, not every guitar is a success, no matter how good the maker; in addition, a guitar bearing a distinguished label may have been modified or otherwise misused, whereas an instrument of more humble origin may have mellowed into greatness. Ultimately it is the sound and playing condition that matter, not the label.

The guitars discussed above are usually hard to obtain and often too expensive for the beginner who is unsure whether he will continue. In this case the choice must be made from mass-produced guitars, which can also reach a high standard. It is a mistake to think of such guitars as factory made, since in general little machinery is employed; more usually the guitars are made by piecework, each workman making one or two parts only and leaving the final assembly to othrs. Often the work is carefully controlled, with a high regard for craftsmanship. The best value for money is unquestionably to be found among the moderately priced Japanese instruments.

Construction of the Guitar

Guitar Woods

The best guitars are almost universally made of the following woods: the back and sides of rosewood, either Brazilian or West Indian; the top of Alpine spruce of close, even grain; the fingerboard of ebony; the bridge of ebony or rosewood; and the neck of cedar or mahogany. Fine guitars sometimes have maple sides and backs, but this is rare nowadays. In less expensive guitars, mahogany and similar hardwoods may be substituted for rosewood, and the fingerboard may be rosewood instead of ebony.

The top—or "table" as it is sometimes called—plays a major part in the sound of the instrument; where possible it is advisable to buy a spruce-topped guitar. The lines of the grain should be close together, if possible, or at least evenly spaced. It is important that the rosewood or ebony fingerboard not be warped; this should be checked by placing a straightedge along it. This can also be checked by holding a string down from the 1st to the 19th frets in which position it should just touch all the frets in between. Figure 2 depicts a test of the fingerboard for straightness.

The Varnish

The final finish given to a guitar has a marked effect on its tone, and good makers invariably finish their instruments by hand with great care. Unfortu-

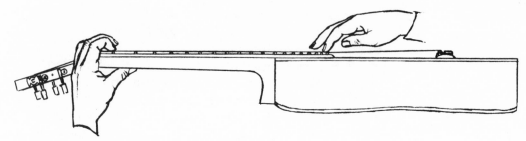

Figure 2. Checking the Neck for Straightness

nately this is not always the case with less expensive guitars, and those having a sprayed on heavy lacquer or plastic finish usually sound much duller and deader for this reason alone. Inexpensive Spanish guitars are usually better in this respect, since lower labor costs permit finishing by hand. In other countries only the most expensive guitars are finished by this method. However, this type of finish, usually shellac-based, is more delicate and liable to watermark.

Cracking

Many people are under the mistaken impression that the better a guitar the less likely it is to crack. There is a germ of truth in this, in that a guitar made of green, unseasoned wood may well crack as the wood dries out; but such guitars should never even be on the market. Otherwise, the better guitar is liable to be more delicate: first, because the wood is often thinner and the construction more delicate for tonal reasons; second, because the finish applied by a good maker is chosen more for its acoustic qualities than for its resistance to climatic changes or rough handling. The good maker rightly expects the owner of a fine instrument to take proper care of it. The commercial producer, on the other hand, is concerned with guaranteeing his product and having as few returns as possible, and so often uses thicker wood heavily sprayed with lacquer, at considerable sacrifice to the tone. Do not be deterred, therefore, by stories of the fragility of certain types of guitar; they may have a better sound. (You will find a section below on the care of your guitar.)

Interior Construction

All good guitars have a form of bracing underneath the table known as fan-strutting (depicted in Figure 3). These struts, which may originally have been added simply for strength, were found to produce a marked improvement in tone quality and became a standard construction technique. The innovation is attributed to Antonio de Torres, a fine maker of the last century; since Torres many minor variations in strutting have been made, the precise pattern being the hallmark of the individual maker.

It is possible to feel for the struts inside a guitar by reaching inside the soundhole, and it is a good idea to check this when buying a guitar.

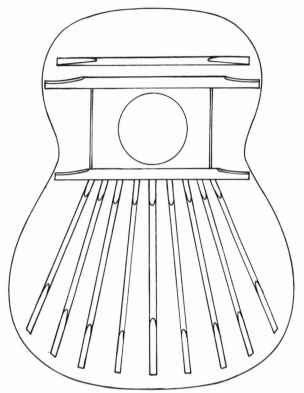

Figure 3. Fan-Strutting Beneath the Table

The Fingerboard

It is most important when buying a guitar to ascertain that the fingerboard is both flat and of sufficient width. Some guitars have a slight bow to the fingerboard, so that it is slightly higher in the center and tapering off at the sides. Although some fine guitars have been made with this type of fingerboard, the curve does not assist technically and is not recommended.

The standard width for the fingerboard is from 2 to 2⅛ inches at the nut, widening slightly and evenly throughout its length to about 2¾ inches at the soundhole. A narrower fingerboard makes playing more difficult, and should be avoided. As in playing the piano, the fingers should be trained to the correct distances; it is a mistake to try to adapt the instrument to the fingers.

Strings

Nowadays the correct strings for the Spanish guitar are made of nylon, which has completely replaced gut on account of its greater durability. The 1st, 2nd, and 3rd strings are usually a single filament, although some sets are available with a thin plastic winding around the 2nd and 3rd strings. The 4th, 5th, and 6th strings consist of a core of thin nylon filaments around which is wound copper wire plated with a silver, gold, or bronze alloy. The silver-plated strings are the most widely used and easily obtained, although good strings are also made of the other alloys and even of solid silver windings.

Steel strings are louder, but that is where their advantage ends, since they are much harder to finger and place an excessive strain on the bridge unless the guitar is especially reinforced. Of necessity they are used on electric or "rhythm" guitars, but these are especially built to accommodate them, whereas the Spanish guitar is not.

Among the many brands, Concertiste, Savarez, Aranjuez, La Bella, and Augustine may be mentioned for their high quality.

String Height

The height of the tightened strings above the fingerboard is important since it governs the playing action of the instrument. If the strings are set too high, the action will be stiff for the left hand, making the guitar hard to play. If, on the other hand, the strings are too low, they will buzz against the frets. Adjustments can be made by raising or lowering the bone pieces at the bridge and nut — an operation that can be done at home but is best left to the experienced repairman or maker.

The Flamenco Guitar

The differences between the flamenco and classical guitar are shown in Figure 4. In general the construction is very similar, though the body of the flamenco guitar is sometimes thinner. The main difference in the sound comes from the use in the flamenco of Spanish cypress wood for the back and sides, which tends to give the instrument a sharper, more brilliant tone, with the sacrifice of some depth and mellowness. The traditional peg tuning is somewhat more difficult to master, and is in fact no longer universally used. It has the advantage that the strings can be changed more quickly, and—some people claim—that the sound is better, but this is by no means proved. On either side of the soundhole are two plates, generally of plastic, to protect the wood from the tapping of the fingernails in the *golpe* stroke.

Undoubtedly flamenco music sounds better on this kind of guitar; but since few are made outside Spain and inexpensive ones are scarce, the beginner is advised to wait until he is sure that he wishes to specialize in flamenco before buying it.

Care of the Guitar

As mentioned above, the better the guitar, the more care it probably needs; therefore the following points should be carefully noted. Because of its large surface-area of thin wood, the guitar is more delicate and accident-prone than, for instance, the violin, a fact that accounts for the rarity of antique guitars. It is safest, therefore, to obtain a strong case for your instrument and keep it in its

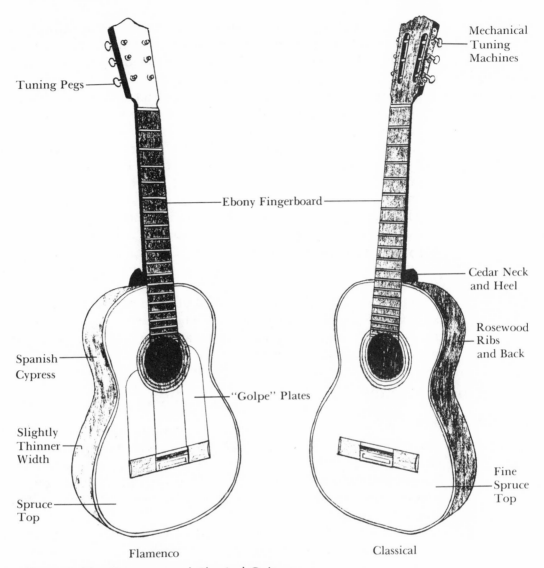

Figure 4. The Flamenco and Classical Guitars

case when not in use. Most cases can also be locked, thereby protecting the contents from the exploring hands of, say small children.

Perhaps the greatest danger to the guitar arises from sharp changes in climate—particularly changes in humidity. In normal humidity the wood of a guitar, however well seasoned, will absorb some moisture; if, however, it is exposed suddenly to extreme dryness through heat, air conditioning, or climatic change it will contract and in severe cases crack or split. This can be avoided by ensuring that the guitar does not become dried out excessively, preferably by keeping a guitar humidifier inside the case and not exposing the guitar to air conditioning (which removes moisture from the air). Nor should the guitar be left in the sun, even though still in its case.

Simple as these rules are, many fine instruments have been damaged through neglect or ignorance of them.

The varnish of a good guitar needs only an occasional rub with a soft cloth to maintain its luster, and should not be waxed. If the varnish is damaged it should be touched up by an expert, and should not be stripped and replaced unless absolutely essential; varnish hardens and improves acoustically with age, and it may be a long time before a revarnished instrument regains it former tone.

Lacquer, on the other hand, may be waxed to increase its luster and provide a protective coat. This should be a thin coat of a hard wax. Care should be taken to avoid touching the strings with it.

If the bass strings begin to sound dull, they can be revived by wiping with a damp cloth or even better, by removing them from the guitar and scrubbing them with soap and water to remove dirt, corrosion, or perspiration. Even relaxing the string for a few minutes will achieve some improvement.

The strings exert considerable tension on the bridge, and therefore should not all be removed together, as the change in tension and stress on the top of the guitar can cause damage in time. The best plan is to change the strings only when necessary, one at a time so as to maintain a more even tension with the other five.

Many people form quite a personal attachment to their guitar after a time, and in that case the few points of care necessary to maintain the instrument in first-class playing condition become a pleasure rather than the chore they might at first appear to be.

Care of the Fingernails

Before starting to play, it is necessary to trim the fingernails of each hand to the correct length. The left-hand nails are cut as short as possible, since otherwise the tips of the fingers cannot reach the fingerboard. The right-hand nails should be filed approximately level with the tips of the fingers, so that when viewed from the face of the hand a very narrow edge shows, following the contour of the finger.

The exact length of the right-hand nails is to some extent dependent upon the individual, since nail formations vary; but experimentation on the above lines will usually achieve the correct length. It is also important not to have a rough edge on the nail, which produces bad tonal effcts; this may be avoided by finishing off the filing with crocus cloth or the finest grade of garnet paper.

Conventional Terminology

Finally, before approaching the next chapter, it is necessary to know how the fingers of each hand are referred to in the text and by convention (see Figure 5).

The letters used for the right hand are derived from the Spanish words *indicio* for index finger, *medio* for middle finger, *anular* for ring finger, and *pulgar* for thumb. For the left hand the numbers 1 to 4 are used, starting with the index finger. In addition, the left and right hands are often referred to as "LH" and "RH" for the sake of brevity. The strings are numbered 1 to 6, the 1st being the thinnest and highest in pitch. Strings 1 to 3 are sometimes known as the "treble" strings and 4 to 6 as the "bass." Note also that reference to a "higher" string always means higher musically, not geographically.

Now it is time to start playing. Good Luck!

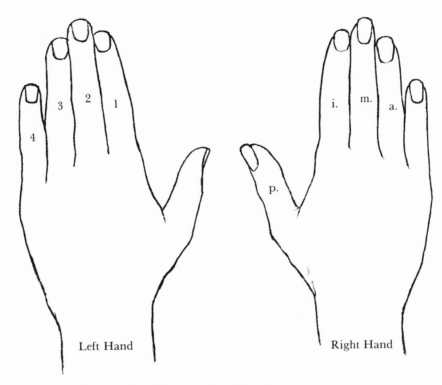

Figure 5. Conventional Finger Identification

CHAPTER TWO

BEGINNING TO PLAY

Stringing the Guitar

When you purchased your guitar it was probably correctly strung with six strings. If this was not the case, however, or if you need to replace a string, Figure 6 shows how the string should be attached to the bridge.

Having knotted the string correctly at the bridge, lead it along the length of the guitar through its correct notch on the nut bone, and thread it through the hole in the tuning-machine barrel. It is a good idea to twist the loose end back around the string, as in Figure 7, so that when you turn the tuning key the tension will first be taken by the twist, and slipping will thus be avoided.

Tuning

Unless you have perfect pitch it will be necessary to buy a pitch pipe or tuning fork in order to tune correctly. Pitch pipes for the guitar are available with six pipes, each giving the pitch of one of the strings. With a little practice you will be able to tighten or loosen the string to correspond with the pitch of its pipe.

Figure 6. Attaching Strings to Bridge

Figure 7. Attaching Strings to Barrel

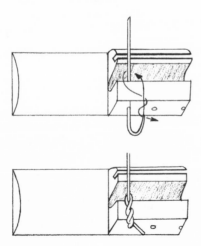

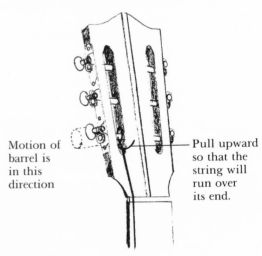

Motion of barrel is in this direction

Pull upward so that the string will run over its end.

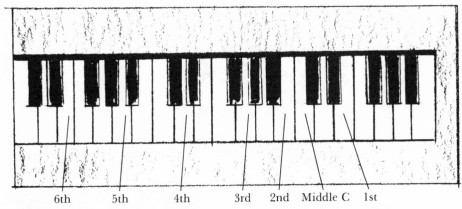

6th   5th   4th   3rd 2nd Middle C 1st

Figure 8. Tuning from a Piano

Alternatively, a piano may be used; Figure 8 shows the equivalent note for each string.

An easy method for checking your tuning is as follows: Press the 6th string just behind the 5th fret with your LH 1st finger, and sound the string with your RH thumb. The note produced should be the same as the 5th string sounded open. (A string is "open" when not pressed down anywhere by the left hand, and therefore is sounding at its natural pitch.)

Now repeat the procedure by placing your LH finger behind the 5th fret of the 5th string; play it, and you should have the sound of the 4th string open. The same procedure on the 4th string gives you the note for the 3rd string open. On the 3rd string only, it is necessary to press behind the *4th* fret to obtain the note for the 2nd string open. On the 2nd string the procedure returns to normal; press behind the 5th fret for the same sound as the 1st string open.

Although many experience difficulty in tuning at first, this is usually overcome by practicing until the habit is formed and the ear trained. All that is necessary is the ability to hear if two notes sound the same. Even if at first you cannot hear whether the second note is slightly sharper (higher) or flatter (lower) than the first, frequent experimentation will train your ear.

Position

In both the body and the hand positions it is of primary importance to be comfortable and relaxed. The standard position illustrated in Figure 9 gives maximum support and firmness in holding the guitar while at the same time allowing the hands to move freely. Note particularly the points stressed in the figure text.

It is hard to overemphasize the importance of acquiring a good position from the start. The standard position, which has been established for many years, has found favor among players for one reason only: In the long run it is the easiest.

Women encumbered by the problems of a tight or short skirt may use the position shown in Figure 10, but it must be emphasized that this is a compromise and not a position favored by the best players. A better performance position for women is illustrated in Figure 11. Alternatively a full skirt may be worn and the Figure 9 position used.

The guitar rests on the left thigh, the leg raised by a small footstool slightly above horizontal position. Right thigh touches guitar and adds support and firmness. Right arm pivots at widest point of the guitar, just below elbow, allowing wrist to hang loosely with knuckles parallel to strings. Left elbow is not held away from body; it hangs naturally at side. Guitar is pulled close to the body and kept upright. Sit on front of chair and lean forward slightly.

Figure 9. Playing Position

Figure 10. Women's Informal Position

Figure 11. Women's Classical Position

The Right Hand

The technique of the right hand can be simply divided into four types of stroke: the *rest stroke*, the *free stroke*, the *chord*, and the *arpeggio*. We will start with the rest stroke—perhaps the most important of all—since the style of a player is very often determined by this technique. The three other strokes will be discussed in following chapters.

The Rest Stroke

1. First, place the tip of the index (*i*) finger so that it touches the 1st string lightly, at the bridge end of the rosette. The finger should be slightly curved.
2. Now, without any other movement, draw the finger across the string so that the fleshy tip then rests on the 2nd string. The nail catches the first string in passing and sounds the note.

This is all there is to the rest stroke, a simple movement if the following points are observed:

1. The finger does not lift from the guitar strings at all, but simply draws across them and slightly down into the space between them.

Figure 12. Right-Hand Position (from Front)

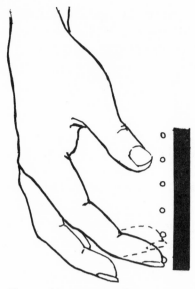

Figure 13. Rest Stroke

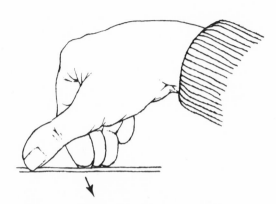

Figure 14. Right-Hand Position (Player's Viewpoint)

2. The hand from the knuckles on back does not move. This is purely a finger movement.
3. *The finger itself does not straighten*, but maintains it natural curve. This is very important, because allowing the finger to yield in this way would take power from the stroke and result in the development of a generally weak touch.
4. Note that the finger does not play quite at a right angle to the string, but is angled to pluck slightly on the left side of the nail as you look down at it (see Figure 14). By varying the angle of the finger it is possible to use more or less nail to engage the string, according to the effect desired. The strongest sounds use more nail, the softest sounds less.

Alternation. An important point to remember is that the rest stroke is almost never repeated on successive notes (even of the same pitch) with the same finger. In scales and single-note runs the fingers alternate to produce the series of notes.

To practice this,

1. Play a rest stroke with the *i* finger on the 1st string.
2. When the *i* finger comes to rest on the 2nd string, repeat the procedure with the *m* finger, placing the tip on the 1st string and drawing it across to rest on the 2nd.
3. As the *m* finger comes across the 1st string, raise the *i* finger again in preparation for the start of another stroke.
4. Now continue these movements, playing the 1st string alternately with the *i* and *m* fingers. Notice that the motion of the fingers is like that of "walking" on the same spot.

Now here is the full exercise: Play the rest stroke, alternating the *i* and *m* fingers, four times on each string, starting at the 1st string with the *i* finger. Remember: Never use the same finger twice in succession. Play the notes slowly and firmly, working your way across the six strings. Do not rest the thumb on the strings, but let it stay loosely beside the index finger. This way you will be more sensitive to what your fingers are doing.

Exercises for the Right Hand

It is now time to learn a simple system of notation for the guitar so that you may play successions of notes without the need for long verbal explanations. The system known a "tablature"—which has been in use in various forms since the sixteenth century—uses six lines, each of which represents one string of the guitar.

If you are to play a certain string open—i.e., without any left-hand fingering—then a "0" is written on the relevant line.

Thus, the example shown means play the 2nd string open, then the 1st.

The exercise you just completed in the previous section would be written as shown.

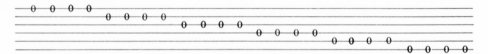

Now try the following exercises, which progressively become slightly more difficult. Play them slowly—and positively—until mastered.

Exercise 1

First: i m i m *etc.*
Then: m i m i *etc.*

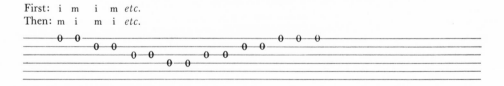

Exercise 2

First: i - m - i m - i - m *etc.*
Then: m - i - m i - m - i *etc.*

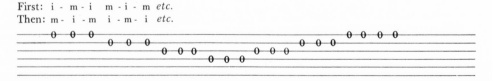

Notice that Exercise 2 is more difficult only because each new string is started with a different finger.

18

Exercise 3

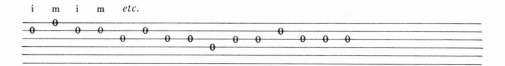

Exercise 4

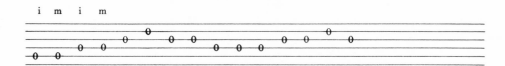

In Exercise 5 you begin using the *a* finger as well. You probably will find alternation between the *m* and *a* fingers more difficult. It is important to develop the strength of the *a* finger in the same way as with the others.

Exercise 5

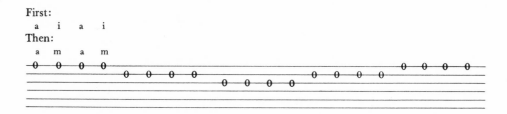

The Left Hand

Although technique for the left hand may not seem as elaborate as that for the right, it is very important to establish and maintain a correct position from the beginning. Study Figure 15 and try to imitate the position. Note:

1. The thumb should rest lightly at the center of the back of the neck. It should be held straight, without any bend at the joint. The point of contact is the ball of the thumb slightly on the side closest to your first finger. *Don't* let the thumb curl round and project beyond the neck of the guitar —one of the commonest faults of beginners.
2. As the left hand moves to play at various points on the fingerboard, the thumb slides with it. The thumb should be positioned almost directly underneath the fret played by the first finger. Actually it is a little forward of that fret—i.e., closer to you. For example, if you are playing frets 1, 2, 3, and 4 on whatever strings, your thumb will be underneath fret 1. If you are playing frets 7, 8, 9, and 10, your thumb will be underneath fret 7.
3. Let your forearm hang down loosely, and keep your elbow in a relaxed position close to the body.

Exercises for the Left Hand

1. Place the 1st finger just behind the 1st fret of the 6th string.
2. Now bring the 2nd finger firmly down behind the 2nd fret of the 6th string, without raising the 1st finger from its position behind the 1st fret.

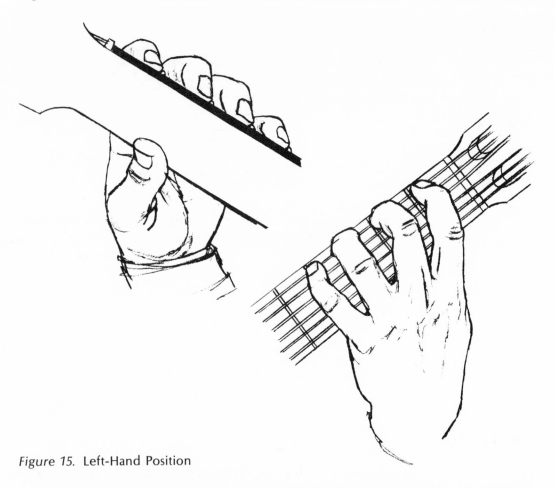

Figure 15. Left-Hand Position

    3. Continue, by placing the 3rd and 4th fingers behind the 3rd and 4th frets respectively. Remember to leave the other fingers in position.

This may seem difficult at first, but it becomes easier as the fingers become accustomed to stretching. Notice that the fingers are nearly vertical to the strings; don't let them lean back.

Now continue the exercise on each string successively (starting at the 6th and progressing to the 1st), placing the four fingers as before. Exercise 6 shows it in tablature. Notice that the numbers of each string refer to frets and not to fingers.

Exercise 6

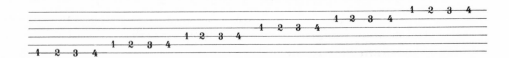

Remember that this exercise is for the left hand alone. As you become accustomed to the movement, it should be possible to hear the sound of each note as your finger strikes it.

If your left hand or wrist becomes fatigued do not continue. Lay the hand flat, with fingers extended, for a moment; this will relax it very quickly.

Both Hands Together

Now is the time to practice all that you have learned in the preceding sections by using both hands together in the next exercise, Exercise 7a. The LH pattern is the same one that you have just practiced.

Exercise 7

(a)
First:
  i   m   i   m *etc.*
Then:
  m   i   m   i *etc.*

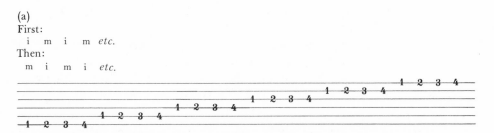

While the LH plays this pattern, the RH is playing the rest stroke (alternating fingers) on the string pressed down by the LH. For one sequence you should begin with the *i* finger, playing *i–m–i–m* on each string; for a second sequence you should reverse this, playing *m–i–m–i*. Always alternate, and remember to leave the LH Fingers in place until you change strings.

Now try coming down, as in Exercise 7b.

(b)

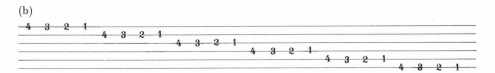

When descending, each LH finger is released as you strike the next, since otherwise only the highest note would sound.

This exercise is progressive; the next stage is to start one fret higher, as in Exercise 7c.

(c)

Following this pattern and starting one fret higher each time, continue until you commence the sequence on the 9th fret (Exercise 7d).

(d)

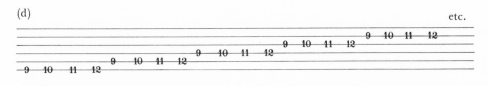

Then begin to descend, starting the next sequence on the 8th fret, until you finally reach your starting position.

This is a famous technical exercise; guitarists in Spain used to have contests (and probably still do) to see who could cover the whole fingerboard first. At this point, however, accuracy and firmness are more important than speed.

Some Common Faults and Their Solution

The notes make an unpleasant buzzing sound. Your LH Finger is not pressing the string just behind the fret, but is in the middle or at the back of the space between the frets. If after you correct this the string still buzzes, your guitar probably needs an adjustment, usually a higher bridge or nut bone.

The notes thud with a dead sound. You are pressing too close to the fret with your LH finger.

The RH finger produces a click before the note sounds. The most likely cause of this problem is that you are starting the stroke too far from the nail tip —i.e., playing too much with the fleshy tip of the finger. Try starting the stroke much closer to the nail tip. Alternatively, you may be playing with the center of the nail instead of angling the finger as explained above in the section on the rest stroke (check Figure 14 again). If the problem still persists, check carefully the section on care of the fingernails in Chapter One.

The sound is too metallic. Your RH is playing too close to the bridge; move it closer to the rosette.

The guitar still doesn't seem correctly tuned. If you still have problems after studying the section above on tuning, try to enlist the help of an experienced musician (not necessarily a guitarist). He will be able to tell you whether you are in tune or not, and help you by practical demonstration.

CHAPTER THREE

BUILDING ACCOMPANIMENTS FROM CHORDS

Two or more notes sounded simultaneously are known as a "chord." As we continue it will be seen that these chordal combinations of notes and the progressions from one combination to another give the characteristic harmony needed to accompany a melody. However, it is necessary to learn and practice some simple chords before learning their practical application.

Playing a Simple Chord

To finger a C chord—the *tonic* chord in the key of C major—

1. Place the 1st finger of the LH behind the 1st fret of the 2nd string;
2. without lifting the 1st finger, place the 2nd finger behind the 2nd fret of the 4th string; and
3. finally, place the 3rd finger of the LH behind the 3rd fret of the 5th string.
4. Now, with the thumb of the RH sweep across the strings from the 5th to the 1st, taking care not to sound the 6th (bottom) string. If your fingers are correctly placed, the sound should be a pleasant full chord. If it is not, check to be sure that the guitar is in tune.

The chord that you have just played can be conveniently depicted as follows:

This diagram represents the first three frets at the end of the guitar fingerboard; the numbers refer to the LH fingers, and the spots show where they are to be placed. The 1st string is on the right. The cross over the 6th string indicates that it is not to be sounded.

Now, following the same principle, try the next chord, as follows. This time sound all the strings.

23

This is known as a G7 chord, and is the *dominant seventh* chord in the key of C major. Again, sweep across the strings with the thumb of the RH.

Changing from One Chord to Another

Most beginners have difficulty at first in changing the left hand from one chord position to another with speed and smoothness. This is mostly a question of practice, but the following rules are important:

1. Move the fingers as little as possible; take the shortest route to the next position.
2. Try to cultivate a smooth, serpentine action with the LH, and avoid jerking or snatching at the strings.
3. Practice chord changes slowly and deliberately until the movements are familiar.

Now try changing from the C chord to the G7 and back to the C, remembering these rules. Notice that each finger has only to travel to an adjoining string; little movement is necessary.

Remember that these first changes will need considerable practice; the LH should be thoroughly used to them before the next section is attempted.

Playing in Meter and Rhythm

Once the LH has become familiar with the C and G7 chords, it is possible to vary the RH fingering so as to more easily play in a rhythm, instead of doing a simple stroke with the thumb. One of the least complicated rhythms to start with is in ¾ meter, the waltz rhythm. It is the rhythm produced when you count evenly out loud, "*One*-two-three, *one*-two-three, *one*-two-three, *one*-two-three," giving a slight stress each time to the "*one*."

To reproduce this on the guitar, place the LH fingers for the C chord. Place the RH thumb ready to play on the 5th string, and the *i*, *m*, and *a* fingers on the 3rd, 2nd, and 1st strings respectively. The fingers should be on their tips, with the nails just in contact with the strings.

1. Counting "*one*" to yourself, stroke down with the thumb to play the 5th string. Let it stay where it comes to rest against the 4th string until it plays again.
2. On the count of "two," stroke up with the RH fingers to sound the 3rd, 2nd, and 1st strings simultaneously. Here, the fingers do not come to rest on the adjacent strings after playing; they just clear the strings and end the movement about ¼ inch above them. This is an example of the *free stroke*.

3. On the count of "three," again pluck the 3rd, 2nd, and 1st strings simultaneously.

Now apply the same procedure to the G7 chord, with the thumb playing the 6th string instead of the 5th. The fingers pluck the first three strings as before.

To complete the exercise play each chord successively in the three-beat waltz rhythm, making the LH change smoothly and without haste.

Exercise 8

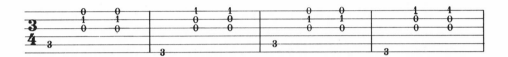

Exercise 8 shows this rhythm in tablature. Notice that each group of three is separated from the next by a vertical line. This is known as a "bar line," and each group of three is known as a "bar" or "measure."

Naturally changes of harmony such as those in Exercise 8 require considerable practice, and before moving on to other chords it is necessary to play them over and over until there is no appreciable pause between measures.

At the same time, however, it is possible using these chords to experiment with different RH "strums," some of which are suggested below.

Simple Thumb Strum

This type of strum has the advantage of being strong and loud, and therefore useful for group singing. It is executed as follows:

1. Place the LH on the C chord.
2. With the RH thumb (*p*) pluck the 5th string as before, letting the thumb come briefly to rest on the 4th string.
3. For the next two beats of the bar sweep the thumb down across the remaining strings, performing the stroke so quickly that the notes sound almost simultaneously.

Exercise 9

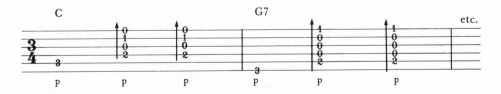

This strum has the advantage of sounding all the notes of the chord; it would be written as in Exercise 9. Note that the G7 chord is played in the same way as the C, the thumb playing first the 6th string and then the remaining strings.

After practicing this in the waltz tempo, try it in $\frac{2}{4}$ time, as in Exercise 10 (a two-beat rhythm). This will take more practice, as the changes come more frequently.

Exercise 10

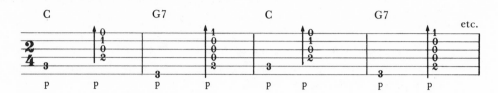

Thumb-and-Fingers Strum

Another useful strum for folk songs uses the thumb in combination with the backs of the nails of the *i*, *m*, and *a* fingers held together.

With a C chord held by the LH, play the 5th string with the thumb. Follow this by a downward nail stroke of the *i*, *m*, and *a* fingernails, held together to make a percussive chord on the remaining strings. The sound is somewhat harsh; but remember that the guitar has a small sound when accompanying a roomful of enthusiastic singers!

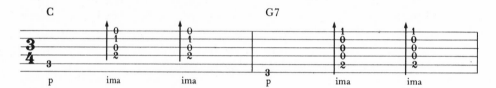

Thumb-and-Index-Finger Strum

Even more useful is a strum using the *i* finger instead of all three, as it can easily be varied into more complex patterns.

In its simple form, this strum is the same as the last one but uses the fingernail of the *i* finger only, instead of the *i*, *m*, and *a* fingers held together.

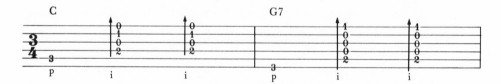

If the *i* finger is pulled back upward across the upper strings after its initial down stroke, it is easy to break up the beats to make a more interesting rhythm.

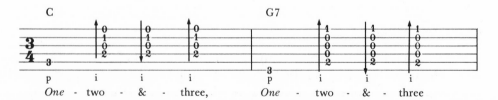

Here the thumb plays the first beat as usual. Then the *i* finger makes a nail stroke, followed quickly by a pull back across the upper strings, all in the second beat. Finally, the *i* finger makes a nail stroke for the third beat. The rhythm of this pattern is *"pom*-tiki-tik, *pom*-tiki-tik," and should be counted out loud as "*one*-two-and three, *one*-two-and-three."

There is almost an infinite variety of RH rhythms used in folk-song accompaniments. It is a good idea to practice and experiment at this point until the RH is accustomed to these strums and the LH is thoroughly familiar with the chord change.

The disadvantage of these strums, as opposed to the original plucking of chords, is that they tend to displace the hand, making it difficult to intersperse arpeggios or single-note runs. For the purpose of a strong rhythmic accompaniment, however, they are very useful; as you encounter each new chord it is a good idea to practice it with a variety of RH strokes until the position and the changes to and from it become thoroughly familiar.

Playing an Accompaniment

Some songs may require only two chords for accompaniment, but the majority require three or more. By learning just one more chord—and practicing the changes to and from it as before—it will be possible to accompany many songs, even at this stage.

The third chord is in this case F, the subdominant chord in the key of C major. To play this chord the 1st finger covers both the 1st and 2nd strings at the 1st fret. (See below, "The Half-Bar," p.42.)

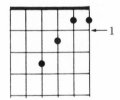

As before, practice the LH alone first, until you can change smoothly to and from both the C and G7 chords.

Then try the waltz rhythm as shown in Exercises 11 and 12, using the RH thumb on the 4th string of the F chord and the three fingers as before.

Exercise 11

Exercise 12

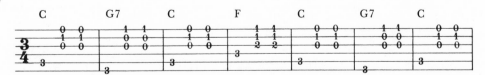

Now for an actual song accompaniment. The tune "On Top of Old Smokey" will most probably be familiar to you, and in a songbook you will usually find the chords indicated like this:

```
    C            F              C
On top of Old Smokey, all covered with snow,
              G7               C
I lost my true lover from courting too slow.
```

This indicates that you start with a C chord, and continue until the "Smo" of "Smokey," at which point you change to the F Chord. Always continue with the same chord until another is indicated.

Exercise 13 has the accompaniment written out in full in tablature.

Exercise 13

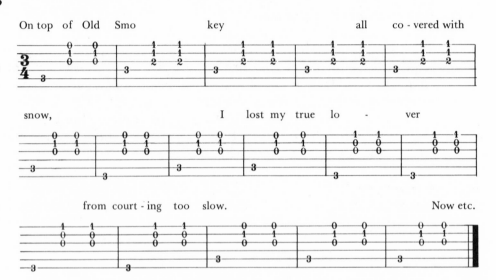

Finally, see if you can accompany the rest of the song from the chord indications alone, keeping strict waltz time.

```
      C          F              C
Now courting's a pleasure, and parting is grief,

              G7               C
And a false-hearted lover is worse than a thief.

      C          F                 C
A thief he will rob you, and take what you have,

              G7                 C
But a false-hearted lover will send you to your grave.

      C          F              C
The grave will decay you, and turn you to dust;

              G7               C
Not one man in a dozen, a poor girl can trust.

        C          F              C
They'll hug you and kiss you, and tell you more lies
```

28

```
            G7                    C
Than cross-ties on a railroad, or stars in the skies.

      C         F           C
So come all you young maidens, and listen to me;

            G7                C
Never place your affections on a green willow tree.

      C         F             C
The leaves they will wither, the roots they will die;

            G7                    C
Your lover will leave you, and you'll never know why.
```

Damping

Having learned the various ways of sounding a chord, we must now learn an important element of technique — how to stop it from sounding! On the piano it is sufficient to raise the hands from the keys; then the notes are automatically "damped" or deadened. On the guitar this is achieved in various ways.

RH Damping

An easy way to stop a vibrating string is to place on it the pad of the RH finger that has just played it. Naturally, this is not practical after executing a rest stroke, as the finger would have to jump from the string below. However, since chords are usually executed with the free stroke — which is better suited to this method — it can often be used with them. The disadvantage lies in the fact that often the fingers will need to move at once to different strings in preparation for the next chord, thereby leaving one or more strings still sounding.

When a chord is played by sweeping the thumb across the strings, the sound may be effectively damped by the fleshy side of the hand opposite the thumb; this can achieve a dramatic effect.

Otherwise we must use LH damping.

LH Damping

If the strings played by the RH are all fingered by the LH the note or chord may easily be damped simply by raising the LH fingers slightly from the fingerboard without losing contact with the strings. If the chord contains an open string, however, it will still sound. In this case you may use the LH 4th finger to damp some or all of the notes, placing it crosswise across the strings. A light touch will be sufficient to deaden the loudest notes; the other fingers should remain in position until they are silenced. Naturally, if the LH 4th finger is being used to finger one of the notes of a chord it cannot also be used to damp it, and in this case one of the other methods must be used.

At this point damping should be a subject for experimentation; later you will find it most useful in eliminating unwanted sounds and particularly effective in emphasizing a marked rhythm.

Use of the Capotasto

The simplest way to raise the pitch of a series of chords to accommodate a higher voice is by use of the capotasto; two of the most frequently used types are illustrated in Figure 16. The capotasto ("capo" for short) is fixed behind any chosen fret, and by shortening the effective string lengths raises the pitch of the whole guitar. Chords are then fingered in the same positions as before, but sound higher in pitch according to the positioning of the capo.

Spanish Type   Standard Type

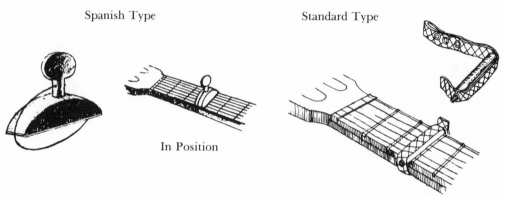

In Position

Figure 16. The Capotasto

Of the two types, the Spanish capo is to be preferred, since it is less cumbersome and can be changed from fret to fret more easily. Where the nylon or gut cord passes around the neck of the guitar it should have a strip of leather as protection against its marking the wood.

The concert guitar rarely utilizes the capo, since it limits the notes available on the fingerboard. In flamenco, however, it is almost invariably used, since the chords are few and depend on the use of open strings for their characteristic sound.

For the simple accompaniment of folk songs—particularly for group singing, where a change of key is often required without the delay of working out new chords—the capo can be most useful in making a few chord patterns go a long way. The main point to remember is not to become dependent on it as a substitute for learning a good variety of chords and using the full range of the guitar.

There is much material in this chapter. Remember that a movement or technique that can be described in a few words may take weeks or months to perfect, so do not be discouraged if you find difficulty at first. Many people who consider themselves fair amateur guitarists never progress beyond the point you have now reached, and may have taken years to reach it through laborious methods of trial and error. Finally, if you still feel awkward and that you have not made progress, reverse the guitar and try playing it left-handed. This will remind you of how you probably felt when you started, and help to gauge your progress.

CHAPTER FOUR

DEVELOPING YOUR TECHNIQUE

Even in simple accompaniments plain, unvaried chords can become monotonous. For this reason it is necessary to develop the technique of the RH so that the harmony can be presented in a more colorful way. In this way the path will be prepared for solo playing.

Exercise 14

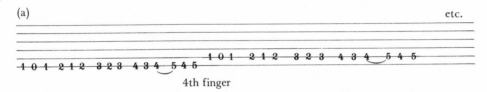

First, it is necessary to improve the single-note (rest stroke) technique learned in Chapter Two. A good development exercise is shown in Exercise 14: with the RH play rest strokes, alternating *i* and *m* fingers; with the LH play the pattern shown. In exercise 14a LH fingering corresponds to the fret numbers except where indicated. To play the 5-4-5 notes, the 4th finger of the LH slides up one fret at the point marked   ; then play the three notes with the 4th and 3rd fingers. Continue the same pattern on each string except the 3rd. When you come to the 3rd string, play only as far as 4-3-4 and then start 1-0-1 on the 2nd string. Your ear will tell you the reason for this.

When you have played 5-4-5 on the top (1st) string, start downward on the pattern shown in Exercise 14b without shifting hand positions. In descending, the 1st finger slides downward at the point marked

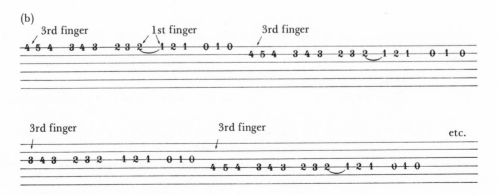

LH fingers should always be left in position where possible, especially if a note is soon to recur. For instance, in playing 1–2–1 on any string the 1st finger should remain in position after playing the first note, to be ready for the third. This is an important general principle which will greatly assist the LH technique.

Practice Exercise 14 slowly at first, playing firm rest strokes with the RH and paying attention to strict alternation of the *i* and *m* fingers. This exercise is excellent for building up strength and security in both hands, and is a good daily practice in warming up.

The Arpeggio

When the notes of a chord are played not simultaneously but one after the other, the pattern is an *arpeggio*. The arpeggio is very useful in accompaniment. You will recall that it is one of the main RH techniques mentioned in Chapter Two.

To execute the arpeggio two points of technique must be observed. First, when the tempo is slow or moderate a rest stroke may be played by the thumb, to give a firm start to the harmonic pattern. As suggested above in the section on the waltz rhythm, this involves the thumb pressing down in toward the guitar to sound the note, and coming to rest on the next string, where it should remain until needed.

Figure 17. Rest Stroke with Thumb

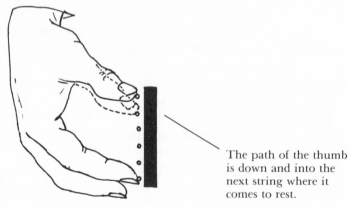

The path of the thumb is down and into the next string where it comes to rest.

When using the fingers, on the contrary, the correct technique here is that of the free stroke. This is best demonstrated through action, so follow these step-by-step instructions:

1. With the LH, finger the C chord.
2. With the RH, place thumb on the 5th string, *i* finger on the 3rd string, *m* finger on the 2nd string, and *a* finger on the 1st string.
3. Press down with the RH thumb to sound the 5th string, leaving it where it comes to rest on the 4th string.
4. Without moving the *m* and *a* fingers, lift out the *i* finger to sound the 3rd string. (The finger does not come to rest.)
5. Without moving the *a* finger lift out the *m* finger to sound the 2nd string.
6. Lift the *a* finger to sound the 1st string.

To repeat the procedure, remember first to place all fingers as in step 2 above. This is a most important rule, as the prior placement of the fingers eliminates many chances for error and enables a clearer and firmer arpeggio to be played.

Exercise 15

p   i   m   a   p   i   m   a   p   i   m   a   p   i   m   a   p   i   m   a

Correct arpeggio technique is quite difficult to play at first, and should be thoroughly and methodically practiced. Exercise 15 gives the above exercise in tablature. For each group of four notes count *"one*-two-three-four," with a slight stress on *"one."* After this has been thoroughly practiced, try Exercise 16, with the LH shift to the G7 chord.

Exercise 16

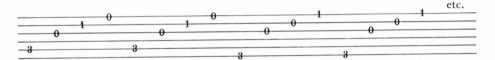

It will be noticed that with some arpeggios it is not always possible to do a rest stroke with the thumb. An example of this is the F arpeggio; in this case the thumb coming to rest against the 3rd string would prevent it being sounded by the *i* finger.

As a general rule, have the thumb play rest strokes when the arpeggio is slow and the string above not needed. Otherwise use the free stroke, letting the thumb curve upward in an arc toward the middle joint of the first finger after sounding the string.

Figure 18. Free Stroke with Thumb

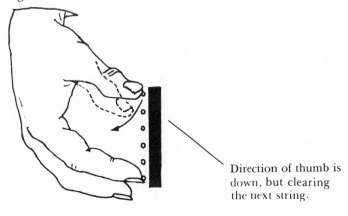

Direction of thumb is down, but clearing the next string.

More Elaborate Arpeggios

The notes of a chord may be played in any order to form an arpeggio, although it is usual to start with the lowest note first. Exercise 17 shows some of the most used patterns. They are arranged in order of difficulty. Remember to practice them slowly, placing all the RH fingers for the chord before commencing the arpeggio. Each two-measure pattern should be repeated continuously until familiar. Play the notes evenly in time, counting *"One*-two-three-four" to coincide with the four thumb strokes in each measure of Exercises 17a and 17b (with ⁴⁄₄ indicated at the beginning). In the same way count *"One*-two-three" to coincide with the thumb strokes in the examples marked ³⁄₄.

Exercise 17

(a)

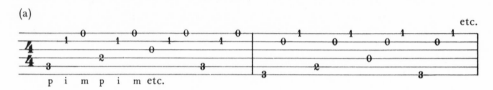

p i m p i m etc.

(b)

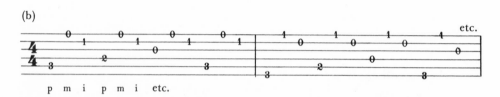

p m i p m i etc.

(c)

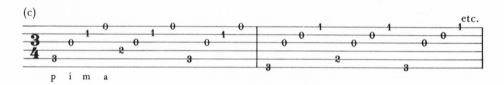

p i m a

(d)

p a m i

(e)

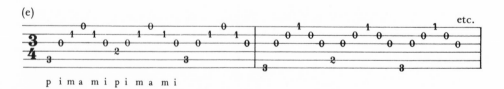

p i m a mi p i m a mi

(f)

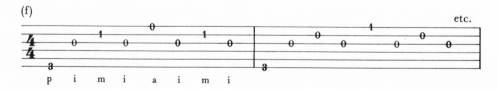

p i m i a i m i

34

Application of the Arpeggio in Accompaniment

As a practical exercise in using the arpeggio, try humming the familiar tune of "Drink to Me Only With Thine Eyes" while playing the following:

Exercise 18

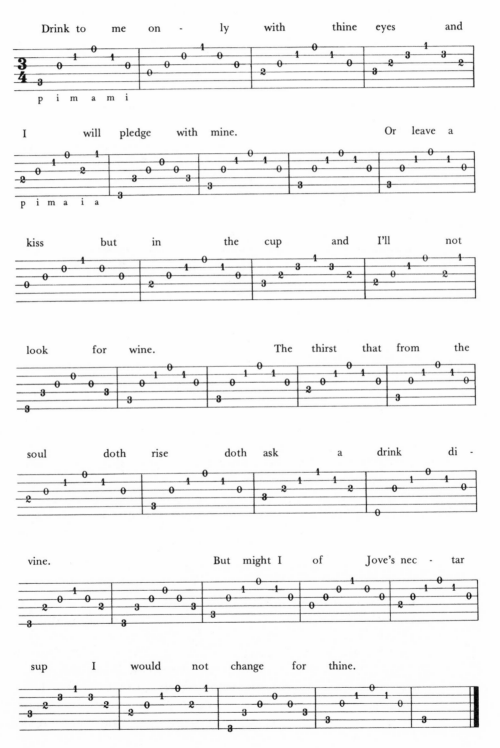

CHAPTER FIVE

CHORD DEVELOPMENT

Assuming that the RH techniques in the previous chapter have been thoroughly practiced, it is now time to extend the range of chord positions familiar to the LH. First, play and learn the names of the following major chords, first strumming them with the RH thumb and then experimenting with thumb-and-three-finger chords and arpeggios:

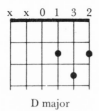

D major

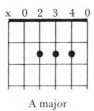

A major

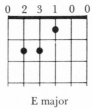

E major

Related Chords

Certain chords bear a special relationship to one another, and fall together in a family, as it were. This is convenient, since it means that to harmonize a song it is not necessary to experiment with all the chords available on the guitar but, in most cases, only with those closely related to the starting chord. Many simple songs rely on only three chords, and the chords you have learned so far have been grouped in threes for this reason. However, it is not necessary to start a song with any given or suggested chord: You may choose another, better suited to the pitch of your voice—providing the relationship of the other chords to the one you select remains the same as in the original.

The main chord, with which you normally start and finish a piece, is known technically as the "tonic" chord. In our original group consisting of C, F, and G7, the C chord was the tonic. The two other, closely related chords are known as the "dominant" and "subdominant"—in this case the G7 and F chords respectively. In the second group, diagrammed above, A is the tonic chord, which makes D the subdominant and E the dominant chord in this particular family. As you read on you will find on p. 52 a chart that enables you to find the dominant and subdominant of any chord you have chosen as your tonic.

The Dominant and Dominant Seventh

Do not be confused by the term "seventh." All this means is that a note—the seventh above the dominant in the scale, (this will be discussed later)—is frequently added to a dominant chord. This gives the dominant chord a characteristic "leading" sound which makes you expect to hear the tonic chord after it. For example, you would not expect to hear a song end like this, with a progression from tonic C to dominant seventh G7:

On the other hand, the progression from G7 to C sounds natural and final:

Athough this is perhaps difficult to understand at first from a verbal explanation, as you play more accompaniments and make up some of your own you will find your ear becoming accustomed to the sound of the dominant seventh, and you will soon feel naturally where and when to use it.

The Subdominant

The subdominant chord is that chord to which the tonic chord is in the position of the dominant, and so for convenience is known as the subdominant. When C is the tonic chord the subdominant is F. To hear this relationship play the progression C, F, G7, C several times.

Minor Chords

So far we have considered only major chords; but many songs are accompanied by minor chords almost entirely, or by a mixture of major and minor. It is therefore necessary to learn some minor chords and train the ear to notice the characteristics distinguishing major from minor.

First play and listen to the sound of the following chords:

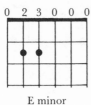 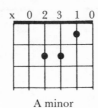 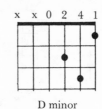

E minor   A minor   D minor

37

As a very general description, one could say that minor chords tend to sound more melancholy, and major chords brighter and more cheerful. As a result, songs with a sad theme are often set in a minor key. However, the difference between major and minor is really something for your ear to discover through your playing of both types of chord and trying to hear the difference.

The Relative Minor

Just as any chord chosen to be the tonic or main chord of a song has as its "family" a dominant and a subdominant chord, so it has also a minor chord particularly associated with it, 1½ tones (1 tone and 1 semitone) below it. This chord is known as the "relative minor." Also likely to be useful are the relative minors of the dominant and subdominant. In the case of C major the relative minor of the tonic is A minor (Am), so the chord family appears as follows:

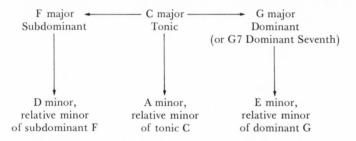

F major	C major	G major
Subdominant	Tonic	Dominant
		(or G7 Dominant Seventh)

D minor,	A minor,	E minor,
relative minor	relative minor	relative minor
of subdominant F	of tonic C	of dominant G

Importance of Chord Families

Having struggled briefly with the theory of the dominant, subdominant, relative minor, etc., you are probably anxious to know the real importance of such knowledge in practical use.

The first and probably most important use is that mentioned above: the assistance such knowledge gives you in harmonizing a tune you have heard. Ultimately you must train your ear to hear which chord sounds right at any point in a melody, but it will help you greatly to know the half dozen most likely chords to try.

Second, this knowledge will help you greatly in transposing a song from one key to another. This is further explained in the next chapter (where you will have widened your range of chords by learning a new technique known as the bar). For the moment, however, let us learn and use in practice the chord families that can be found without using the bar, concentrating on the tonic, dominant (or dominant seventh), subdominant, and relative-minor chords.

Key of G

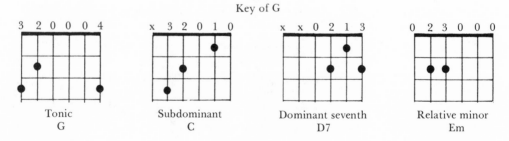

Tonic	Subdominant	Dominant seventh	Relative minor
G	C	D7	Em

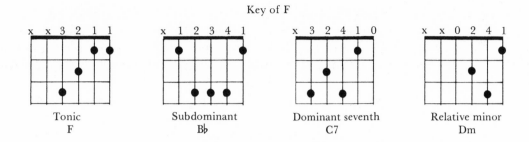

Key of F

| Tonic
F | Subdominant
B♭ | Dominant seventh
C7 | Relative minor
Dm |

In Appendix 1 you will find familiar tunes to use in practicing these chords. If you do not know a melody, try to obtain the help of someone who can read music.

First, however, it is necessary to increase the RH chord technique by learning how to use thumb and fingers simultaneously to play a chord.

Complete RH Chord Fingering

So far, chords have been played either with a simple thumb strum stroke across the strings or by using thumb and fingers successively. To play with thumb and fingers plucking simultaneously requires practice at first, particularly to ensure a minimum of movement and avoid "grabbing."

Since this technique permits the playing of only four strings at a time—whereas chord symbols often show a possible five or six notes—it is necessary to select the four notes of the chord that sound best in the particular context. For example, the 5th, 3rd, 2nd, and 1st strings could be selected for the C chord:

1. With the LH finger the C chord.
2. With the RH place the thumb and fingers on the 5th, 3rd, 2nd, and 1st strings as if to commence an arpeggio.
3. Without lifting the RH more than a fraction, let the fingers pluck back and up as the thumb sweeps forward and down. Both thumb and fingers play a free stroke, and there is a very slight clockwise twist to the hand. (See Figure 19.)

Figure 19. Chord Technique

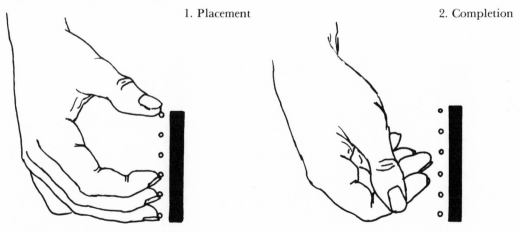

1. Placement   2. Completion

After trying this out on chords you know, read Exercises 19, 20, and 21 slowly and with great attention to the RH. (Note that Exercise 21 combines single notes and chords.) Count a slow "*One*-two-three-four" to each measure. When you see the tie sign (⌒) play the chord only once, and hold it for the additional count.

In connection with the LH fingering it is most important to remember the following rule: Where the same finger is used on the same note in two successive chords, it should be left on the fingerboard to support the hand and facilitate the change. Try to make the LH changes as smoothly as possible. Remember also to place the RH fingers on the strings before playing the chord.

Exercise 19

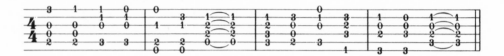

Exercise 20

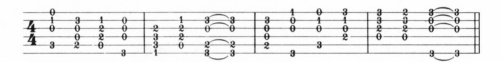

Exercise 21

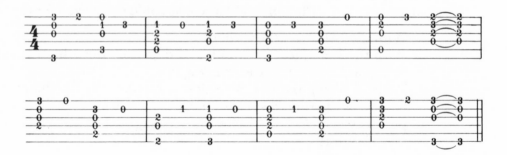

CHAPTER SIX

MORE ADVANCED LEFT-HAND TECHNIQUE

If the preceding chapters have been well practiced and understood, it will now be possible to take a major step forward in technique by learning the bar and the *ligado*. You should carefully study these operations in the step-by-step descriptions that follow, bearing in mind that nobody finds them simple until they have been thoroughly practiced.

The Full Bar

The full bar—also known as the *grand barré* (Fr.), or in Spain, *capotasto*—is a system for fingering chords by placing the LH 1st finger across the strings and using the remaining fingers to form the chord (see Figure 20). Here is an example of a G chord fingered this way:

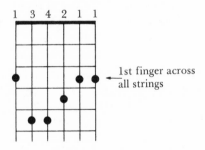

1st finger across all strings

For correct placement of the 1st finger with this chord, follow this procedure:

1. Place the 1st finger across all the strings just behind the 3rd fret, touching them lightly but not pressing them down yet.
2. Locate the LH thumb in the correct position underneath the 3rd fret.
3. Looking at the tip of the LH 1st finger, rotate it a fraction counterclockwise but maintain the line parallel with and just behind the 3rd fret.
4. With the RH, sweep across the strings with the fleshy part of the thumb. This should produce a dampened, dead sound.
5. Continuing this movement with the RH thumb, gradually increase the pressure between LH 1st finger and thumb until a clear, unmuffled sound

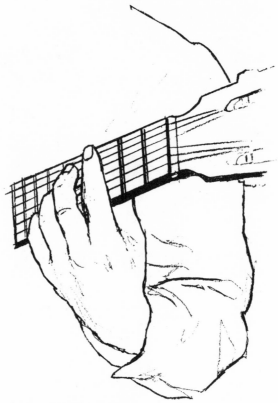

Figure 20. The Full Bar

is heard from all six strings. Do not increase the pressure beyond this point, as it is extremely tiring for the LH. When the 1st finger has reached its correct position, you should just be able to feel the edge of the fret with it. If the finger is too close to the fret, the sound will be deadened; insufficient pressure or a position too far from the fret will produce a buzz.

6. Finally, when the LH 1st finger is placed to your satisfaction, add the other fingers according to the diagram and play the full G chord with your RH thumb.

It is a good idea to practice movements 1–5 behind various frets until you can obtain a clear sound without undue pressure. Then—using Figure 23, the chord chart near the end of Chapter Seven (p. 50)—practice complete chords with the bar.

The Half-Bar

The half-bar—known also as the *petit barré* (Fr.) or *medio capotasto* (It.) —follows the same rules as does the bar, except that only the top four strings are covered by the 1st finger, as in Figure 21. A bar can cover any number of strings, but the contours of the finger make either the complete bar or the four-string half-bar the most satisfactory.

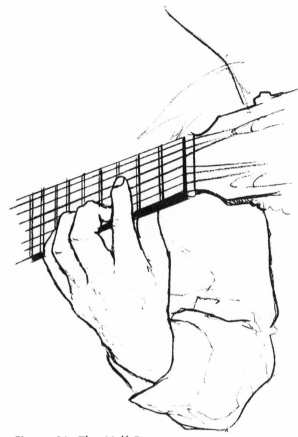

Figure 21. The Half-Bar

The Ligado

The *ligado* is a technique involving the LH, used in sounding more than one note when only one is struck by the RH. *Ligado* in Spanish means "tied," and the expression arises from the notes played in this way sounding more joined together than notes struck individually with the RH. The technique differs for ascending or descending notes, so we will deal with these separately.

The Ascending Ligado

In this technique, also known as the "hammer" or "hammer-stroke," the LH fingers in the usual manner a note played by the RH; but before this note has ceased to sound, another LH finger is brought firmly down on the same string to sound a second note without any additional movement of the RH.

Here is an example:

1. Place the LH 1st finger behind the 1st fret of the 1st string.
2. Play the note with the RH *i* finger.
3. Before the note has ceased to sound, bring the LH 2nd finger smartly down behind the 2nd fret of the same string. This should make a clearly audible note.

Now continue as follows:

1. Place the 3rd finger of the LH behind the 3rd fret of the same string.
2. Play the note with the RH *i* finger.
3. Bring down the LH 4th finger firmly behind the 4th fret to sound the second note.

In tablature the slur mark is used to indicate the *ligado*.

To complete this, continue on all strings as shown in Exercise 22.

Exercise 22

The *ligado* need not, of course, be between adjoining notes only. It can also be from an open string to a fret and can involve many other combinations.

The Descending Ligado

The descending *ligado*, also known as the "pull-off," is executed as in this example (see Figure 22).

Figure 22 about here
FN FC about here

1. Place the LH 1st finger firmly behind the 1st fret of the 1st string, and the 2nd finger behind the 2nd fret of that string.
2. Sound the string with the RH *i* finger. This of course plays the 2nd-fret note.
3. Pull off the LH 2nd finger, pulling the string as you do so to sound the 1st-fret note.

These are the important points to note:

1. The lower finger—in this case the one behind the 1st fret—must be firmly and securely placed before starting the *ligado*.
2. The finger that executes the pull-off must not simply lift from the string but pull down toward the fingerboard.

1. This finger holds the string firmly and does not move.
2. This dotted position indicates the placement of the second finger before the pull-off motion. The second finger as well as the first should be placed firmly.
3. Final position of second finger after pulling off.

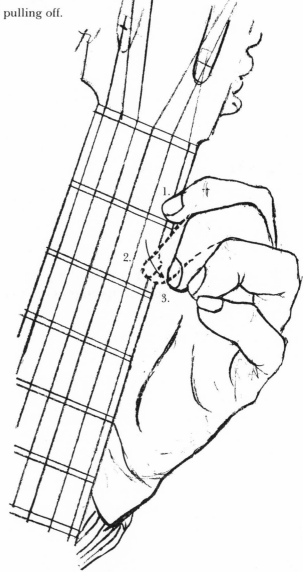

Figure 22. Descending Ligado

3. If the pull is made sideways—i.e., along the same line as the fret—the note is liable to sound too thin and tinny. This can be overcome by pulling slightly at an angle toward the nut of the guitar.

Exercises 23 and 24 provide further *ligado* practice. Each should be practiced on all strings. Exercise 24 combines ascending and descending *ligados*.

Exercise 23 (a)

(b)

(c)

Exercise 24

The techniques in this chapter are most important and should be thoroughly practiced before you proceed to the rest of this book.

CHAPTER SEVEN

WHAT YOU HAVE LEARNED, AND HOW TO PERFECT IT

The purpose of the previous chapters has been to give you an outline of the basic techniques of guitar, all before approaching the problems of reading music, complicated time-keeping, and so on. Of these techniques, the rest strokes of fingers and thumb and barré probably have presented the greatest difficulty; they will now need the most practice. Because of the limitations of tablature notation it is not possible to present elaborate studies for your practicing, nor is it even advisable; at this stage it is more important for you to give full attention to the mechanics of playing than to decipher elaborate studies. For this reason the following suggestions are made to guide you in your technical practice.

Techniques

The Rest Stroke

Do not limit yourself to one part of the fingerboard, but experiment all over the guitar. Pay particular attention to producing clear notes free from buzzing; exercise the *a* finger to the same extent as the others, since this will greatly increase your general dexterity.

To make this more interesting, try playing tunes you know well, experimenting with them on different parts of the fingerboard. As well as increasing your general knowledge of the guitar, this will assist in training your ear—an important feature of musicianship.

Arpeggios

Arpeggios can be practiced in conjunction with learning new chords and chord changes, and also of course in song accompaniment. Remember particularly not to "pick at" the notes; prior placement of the RH fingers will assist you in avoiding this. Do no feel limited to the patterns already given in this text; there are many possible arpeggio combinations which you can find by experiment.

The Bar

Nobody pretends that the bar is easy to play at first, but it can be mastered if the following points are constantly borne in mind.

1. If you seem to be having no success, and your left hand is becoming strained, stop for a moment and go back to the very first principles. If you are practicing the position wrong, no amount of repetition will help and the left hand will soon tire. To rest it, spread your fingers out on a flat surface for a few moments.
2. Remember that the fault may lie with the other fingers, not the bar finger. Many beginners who cannot sound a clear barred chord mistakenly increase the pressure on the bar finger when the other fingers are in fact causing the problem.
3. Remember that minimum pressure consistent with clarity is the ideal—spare your left hand where possible!

Ligados

As with the rest stroke, *ligados* should be practiced all over the fingerboard. They constitute excellent physical training for the left hand. Attention should be given to making a smooth rather than abrupt joining of the notes. Practice particularly with the 3rd and 4th fingers, which are naturally weaker and need more exercise.

Chords

Figure 23 ("Chord Chart," pp.50-51) gives the main common chords of the guitar, with alternative positions in some cases. There are many more possible combinations, but at this point it is better to avoid undue complication. Notice how many new chords become available when you move your barring finger.

These common chords are sufficient for the accompaniment of most folk songs. The more complex chords—such as minor sevenths, ninths, and so on—usually entail only the addition or alteration of one note to change the "flavor" of a chord; examples of these are given at the end of the book. For the moment concentrate on mastering the common chords, which are the heart of song accompaniment, and on understanding the relationships between them.

Notation of Chord Sequences

When a song has many verses following the same chord pattern, it is sometimes convenient to write the sequence out in short form. This is customarily done by drawing vertical lines to indicate the measure and inscribing the chords in the sequence in which they occur. Although each measure contains its normal number of beats, these are not all written in if the chord does not change. For instance, in a four-beat measure where a C chord is to be played four times, the sequence could be written thus: | C C C C |. More usually, however, it would be simply written | C |. If there is a chord change within the measure, this must be written between the vertical lines. Thus, | C G C G | C | indicates two full measures, the first changing chords on each beat, the second with a C chord throughout played four times. If a four-beat measure contains one chord on the first two beats and another on the second two (each chord played twice), it is usually written thus: | C : G |.

Here are some examples of chord sequences written this way:

Careless Love

$\frac{4}{4}$ | F | C7 | F | F |
F	D7	G7	C7
F	F7	B♭	B♭m
F	C7	F	F

12-Bar Blues (in A)

$\frac{4}{4}$ | A | D7 | A | A7 |
| D | Dm | A | A |
| E7 | D7 | A:D7 | A:E7 |

When the Saints Go Marching In

$\frac{4}{4}$ | A | A | A | A |
A	A	E7	E7
A	A7	D	D
A	E7	A	A

Figure 24 ("Chord Clock") is intended to help you both in transposing songs from one key to another to suit your voice and in learning the related chords within any key. Using it is simple: Suppose you wish to accompany a song written in C—but it is too low for you, so you wish to put it up to D. On the "clock" D is "ten minutes after" C, so all the chords of the song can be in sequence transposed simply by counting clockwise ten minutes. For example, suppose the chords are C, Am, F, Dm, G7, C. Counting round in each case, C becomes D, Am becomes Bm, F becomes G, G7 becomes A7, and C again becomes D. The new sequence can then be written out or the necessary alteration made on the music. To test yourself, try writing out the chord sequences in the above songs starting on E, C, and F respectively.

In addition, you will find that with the chord clock the related chords for any chord can be easily found by the following method: "five minutes forward" from any chord gives its dominant, "five minutes back" is subdominant. Immediately inside the circle is each chord's relative minor. Taking, for instance, the key of B♭, this gives F as the dominant, E as the subdominant, and Gm, Dm, and Cm as the respective minors. With these chords you will be well on the way to harmonizing a song in the key of B♭.

Assuming that you have worked methodically through these first chapters and have thoroughly practiced the techniques described, it is now time to learn proper musical notation. You will find few technical problems in the next

Figure 23. Chord Chart

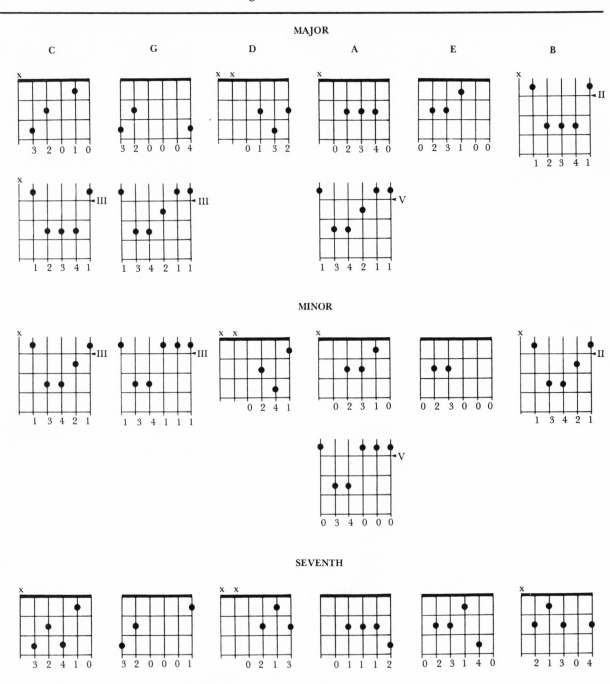

Roman numerals show the fret behind which to place your bar.

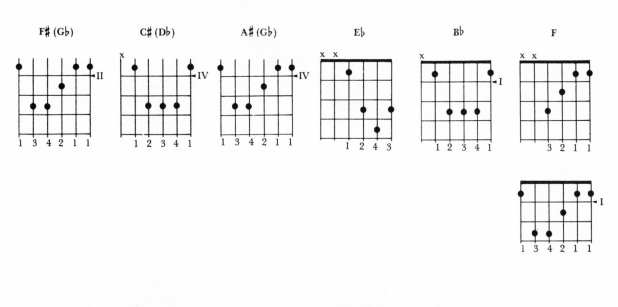

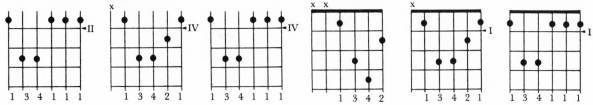

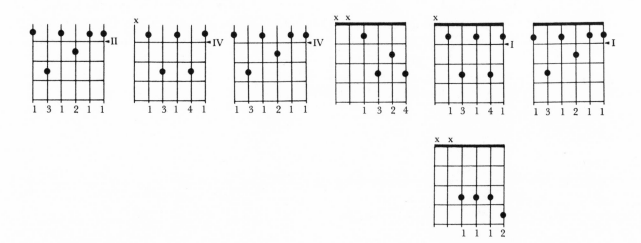

m = minor

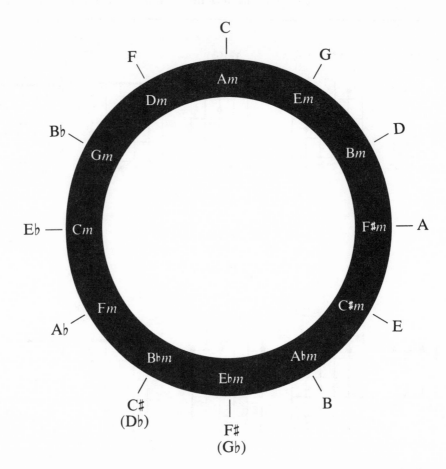

You will have noticed by now that there is no difference between some notes—for instance, C♯ and D♭ —on the guitar, and therefore that many keys could be named two ways. However, usually one of the two is much more commonly used, and these more widespread terms are shown above, except where both namings are in reasonably common use.

Figure 24. Chord Clock

chapters, and can therefore concentrate fully on learning the various symbols used and understanding their meanings. If you still feel uncertain about any of the techniques, go back to first principles—you may have missed a sentence that will solve the whole problem. Remember that hand positions and habits learned at this stage will be difficult to unlearn later, so now is the time for scrupulous checking and revision.

CHAPTER EIGHT

READING MUSIC FOR THE GUITAR

Standard musical notation for both the guitar and the other instruments is written on what is known as a "staff," consisting of five lines with four spaces between them. Each line and each space represents a rung on the musical ladder from the lowest to the highest note, and the first thing to learn is the note which each line or space represents.

The Treble Clef

E F G A B C D E F

The sign at the left-hand end of this staff is that of the treble clef, which is always used for guitar music. The clef sign shows where, on the complete imaginary ladder of notes, this staff has been located so as to contain most of the notes we normally play on the instrument.

The example above shows the notes of the staff in succession, but they are most easily memorized as follows:

1. The lines, from the bottom up, represent E, G, B, D, and F or, as the old memory aid goes, "*Every good boy does fine.*"
2. The spaces, from the bottom up, represent F, A, C, and E, which is easy enough to remember.

Since the range in notes of most instruments is more than the range of the staff, small lines are drawn for higher or lower notes when necessary. These are known as "ledger" (or "leger") lines.

G A B C

D C B A

The lines and spaces continue to repeat the first seven letters of the alphabet upward and downward as far as is necessary to include every note that can be played on the instrument. In the case of the guitar the extremes are E and B.

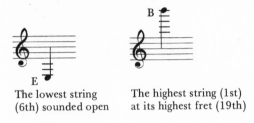

The lowest string
(6th) sounded open

The highest string (1st)
at its highest fret (19th)

Octaves

You will notice that only seven letters are used for notes: A through G. When a note occurs again after seven notes it is known as the same note an "octave" higher; and the range of eight notes together is an "octave." The higher note, which bears the same letter name as the lower one, has the same tonal sound; it is simply higher. To demonstrate this, take the guitar and play the following notes:

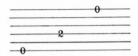

These notes all bear the letter-name "E" and would be written musically thus:

They are the same note with an octave's separation between them.

Note that all guitar music is written one octave higher than it sounds, so that all notes may be written on or near the treble clef staff.

The Open Strings

Having learned the notes on the staff, the next stage is to learn where these are to be found on the guitar. First of all, the names and notes of the open strings should be well memorized.

54

After these become thoroughly familiar, try reading Exercises 25 and 26. Counting an even four for each measure, continue until you can play through evenly with no gaps or pauses.

Exercise 25

Exercise 26

Time

The length of time a note is to last is indicated by the way the note symbol is drawn. Here are the main units:

	American	*English*	*Equivalences*
𝅝	whole note	semibreve	
𝅗𝅥·	dotted half note	dotted minim	𝅗𝅥· + 𝅗𝅥 = 𝅝
𝅗𝅥	half note	minim	𝅗𝅥 + 𝅗𝅥 = 𝅝
𝅘𝅥	quarter note	crochet	𝅘𝅥 + 𝅘𝅥 = 𝅗𝅥
𝅘𝅥𝅮 (𝅘𝅥𝅮𝅘𝅥𝅮)	eighth note(s)	quaver(s)	𝅘𝅥𝅮 + 𝅘𝅥𝅮 = 𝅘𝅥
𝅘𝅥𝅯 (𝅘𝅥𝅯𝅘𝅥𝅯)	sixteenth note(s)	semiquaver(s)	𝅘𝅥𝅯 + 𝅘𝅥𝅯 = 𝅘𝅥𝅮
𝅘𝅥𝅰 (𝅘𝅥𝅰𝅘𝅥𝅰)	thirty-second note	demisemiquaver	𝅘𝅥𝅰 + 𝅘𝅥𝅰 = 𝅘𝅥𝅯

Counting Time

To simplify the process of playing in time, the staff is divided by vertical lines (as shown above with tablature) known as "bar lines." The number of units in each measure remains throughout the same as indicated at the beginning of the first line, just after the clef sign. For instance, the waltz time studied in Chapter Three is known as ¾ ("three-four"), since each measure contains three quarter notes. A measure in ¾ could, however, contain any of the following combinations:

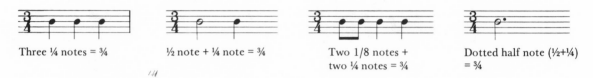

Three ¼ notes = ¾   ½ note + ¼ note = ¾   Two 1/8 notes + two ¼ notes = ¾   Dotted half note (½+¼) = ¾

In fact the notes within a bar in ¾ may have any time value, providing the total is equivalent to three quarter notes.

The easiest way to keep time and give each note its correct value is to count the beats of the measure. Using the same example—which has of course three beats per measure—count as follows:

One - two - three,   One - two - three   One - & - two - three   One - two - three

Notice that when there is more than one note per beat, as with the eighth notes above, the extra note is counted by saying "and" between the main counts.

One - & - two - & - three,   One - two - & - three,   One - two - three-&,   One - two-three,

The main counts of "One-two-three" must be absolutely even, with no pause between the bars. It may help to tap your foot in time with these main counts.

Now let us return to the guitar and play Exercise 27 in time, counting the rhythm. Thumb strokes should be rest strokes, finger strokes free strokes.

Exercise 27

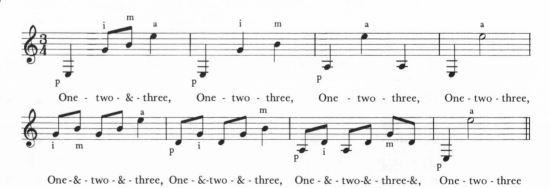

One - two - & - three,   One - two - three,   One - two - three,   One - two - three,

One - & - two - & - three, One - & -two - & - three, One - & - two-& - three-&,   One - two - three

Fretted Notes

The open strings by themselves tend to sound dull, so now we will learn some fretted notes with which to practice time and note reading.

Notes on the 1st, 2nd, and 3rd Strings

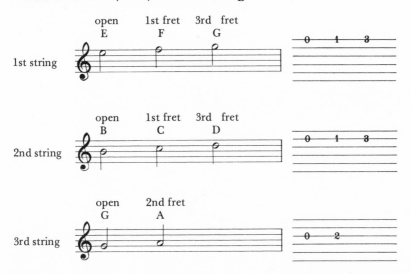

Exercise 28 is in $\frac{4}{4}$ time—that is to say, four counts to the bar, each count a quarter note. $\frac{4}{4}$ time is the most widely used meter, and is therefore also known as "common time." It is often indicated just by a large C, thus:

Notice particularly that the numbers beside the notes in Exercises 28–37 indicate the LH fingers, *not* the frets. This is standard procedure, and will be observed from here on.

Exercise 28

Exercise 29

57

Exercise 30

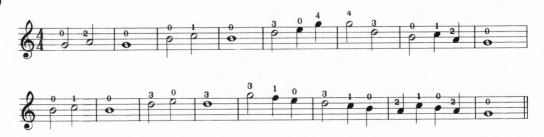

Exercise 31

Exercise 32

Exercise 33

Notes on the 4th, 5th, and 6th Strings

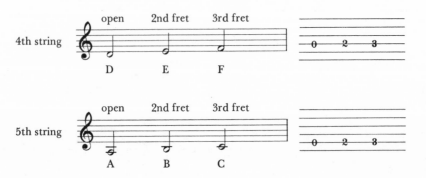

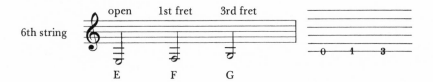

6th string

open — 1st fret — 3rd fret

E   F   G

Exercise 34

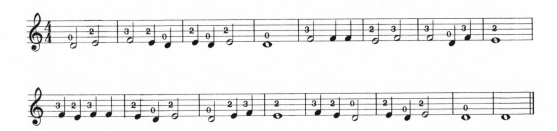

Exercise 35

Exercise 36

Exercise 37

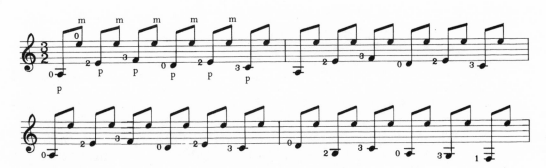

59

Exercise 37 cont.

Music in Two Parts

When you feel familiar with the notes given so far, it becomes time to start reading music with more than one part. This is more difficult at first, but because even simple chords add harmony the music sounds more full and interesting.

In a measure each part by itself will add up to the complete time of the measure, so do not be confused by seeing apparently too many notes per measure.

The top part (with the stems up) contains four quarter notes, equalling $\frac{4}{4}$. The bottom part (downward stems) contains one half note, two eighth notes, and one quarter note: $\frac{1}{2} + \frac{2}{8} + \frac{1}{4} = 1$ or $\frac{4}{4}$.

Counting Two Parts

Once the concept is grasped by counting beats rather than notes, it is as easy to count music in two parts as in one. In this measure in $\frac{4}{4}$ time, for instance, with mixed quarters and eighths in two parts, each beat is given a number count, with an "and" for each eighth note in either line:

One - & two three four - &

First count the above without playing: Then try counting and playing together. Note that the F in the lower part on the first beat must be held through to the

60

second beat; similarly the C in the upper part on the last beat must remain held while both the E and F are played.

As other time values appear, simply remember the following:

1. Count each beat.
2. Hold any longer note for its full time value.
3. Use the "and" approach to divide the beat where necessary for eighth notes.

Exercise 38 gives some simple examples for counting and playing. Try to see why the count is as shown.

Exercise 38

Many beginners, when first playing two-part melodies, experience difficulty in deciding where to use rest or free strokes with the fingers or thumb. In fact, most chords can be played free stroke with both finger and thumb. However, for the purpose of accentuating the melody part, the rest stroke is sometimes used for the upper line, particularly on the accented beat at the beginning of a measure. Thus, a melodic passage is usually played with the rest stroke even though only a single bass note be sustained underneath it. This is demonstrated in Exercise 39, where the letter "r" over a note indicates a suggested rest stroke. Here the melody is in the upper part.

Exercises 40 and 41—with the melody respectively in the upper part and in both parts—show the type of two-part music that would normally be played with free strokes throughout. In Exercise 40 the bass should be emphasized to bring out the melody, but a firm free stroke is usually sufficient for this purpose, due to the greater natural volume of the lower three strings. For this reason—and because of the usual upper position of melody—there is a tendency to use rest strokes more on the upper two strings than on the lower ones. But it is not usual to follow an absolutely consistent pattern, as this would tend to make the music sound mechanical. The best overall advice that one can give is for you to experiment freely so as to develop judgment as to what sounds best in a particular situation.

Exercise 39

Exercise 40

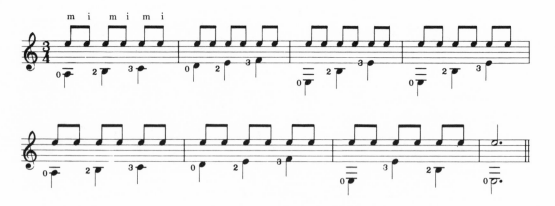

Exercise 41

Additional Symbols

Rests

Since each measure must contain its full quota of time value, when any line of music is silent a sign is put in to show the length of this silence. The symbols correspond in time to those for notes.

▬ whole rest	(**o**)		ꞋꞋ eighth rest	(♪)
▬ half rest	(𝅗𝅥)		ꞋꞋꞋ sixteenth rest	(♬)
𝄽 quarter rest	(♩)		ꞋꞋꞋ thirty-second rest	(♬)

Exercise 42

Exercise 43

Exercise 44

Ligados

Ascending and descending ligados are indicated with a curved line (⌒) similar to that used for them in tablature. Be sure to play the ligados in measures 5, 6, and 7 of Exercise 45.

Exercise 45

CHAPTER NINE

SHARPS AND FLATS

The Scale

You will have noticed in learning the notes in the preceding chapter that the interval between adjacent notes has in some cases been a distance of one fret, in others of two. On the guitar each fret represents an interval of half a *tone*, and two frets an interval of a whole tone. From one note to another may therefore be either a tone or a semitone (as half a tone is called). This is how the notes are separated:

^C tone ^D tone ^E semitone ^F tone ^G tone ^A tone ^B semitone ^C

These notes played in succession are known as a "major scale." The scale following this pattern of tones and semitones is that to which our ears are the most accustomed. Play it on the guitar and you will notice how familiar it sounds.

These are the notes we use when playing in the key of C—that is to say, playing melodies accompanied by the C chord and its related chords. Up to now there has been no need to use the extra semitones that lie between the notes.

Suppose, however, that we wish to play a song in the key of G, using the G chord as our tonic. If we used the same notes as in the C scale, the important pattern of tones and semitones would be lost. Starting on G, we would have the following pattern:

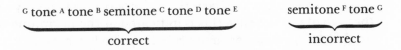

Since from E to F is only a semitone, the correct pattern of tone-tone-semitone-tone-tone-tone-semitone has been lost above the E. For the pattern to be correct and therefore sound right to our ear, we must play a whole tone be-

65

tween E and F and a semitone between F and G. This is done by "sharping" the F—which means in fact using not the F but the semitone above it, known as "F sharp."

Sharps

On the guitar, the sharp is always one fret (one semitone) above the note sharped.

6th string

F   F#
1st fret   2nd fret

4th string

F   F#
3rd fret 4th fret

1st string

F   F#
1st fret   2nd fret

Now play the G scale and notice that it has the same familiar sound as the C scale, although at a different pitch.

Try playing it without the sharped F, and you will notice the difference.

Key Signatures

Since it is necessary to sharp the F every time when playing in the key of G, for the sake of convenience this is indicated at the beginning of the musical line after the clef sign, rather than every time the F occurs:

This sign at the beginning of a line means that you should sharp every F unless a contrary indication is given. An additional advantage of this is that it enables you to tell at a glance in what key a piece is written; it is therefore known as the key signature.

Naturals

If a composer wishes to negate the sharping of a note—for instance, when changing key within a piece—a "natural" sign (♮) is written before the note.

This natural sign affects the remainder of the measure, but not the next measure.

F natural   F sharp

In the above example, if the composer had wished the second F in the bar to be sharp again this would have been indicated thus:

Flats

To make a scale in any key it is only necessary to preserve the same sequence of tones and semitones. When a note must be reduced by a semitone—for instance, to make a semitone interval at the correct point when the succeeding note is a whole tone away—this reduction is known as "flatting" the note.

In the key of F, for example, we require a semitone above A to preserve the pattern. But A to B is a whole tone, so the B is flatted one semitone to B♭. On the guitar, the flatted note is one fret below its natural counterpart.

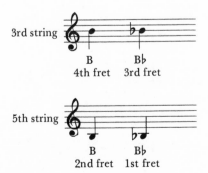

3rd string

B   B♭
4th fret   3rd fret

5th string

B   B♭
2nd fret   1st fret

The B on the 3rd string is, of course, the same note as the 2nd string played open. It is shown here in this position to demonstrate its relationship to the flatted note.

The key signature of F is written thus:

This is the F scale written over two octaves:

Completion of the First Two Positions

Figure 25 shows the complete notes of the first five frets of the guitar. Frets 1 through 4 are known as the *first position* and frets 2 through 5 as the *second position*. Each of the positions on the guitar is given the number of its lowest fret

Figure 25. Complete Notes of First Five Frets (First and Second Positions)

	1		2		3		4		5
E	F		F♯	G♭	G		G♯	A♭	A
B	C		C♯	D♭	D		D♯	E♭	E
G	G♯	A♭	A		A♯	B♭	B		C
D	D♯	E♭	E		F		F♯	G♭	G
A	A♯	B♭	B		C		C♯	D♭	D
E	F		F♯	G♭	G		G♯	A♭	A

Sharps and Flats

—covered by the first finger—and includes the succeeding three frets, covered by the other fingers.

Use these notes to play Exercises 46–49, remembering that

1. sharps or flats at the beginning of a line just after the clef sign comprise the key signature, and whenever these notes are encountered, in whatever octave, they must be sharped or flatted; and
2. a sharp or flat at any other point applies to that note and other occurrences of that note only for the remainder of the measure in which it occurs.

Exercise 46

Exercise 47

Exercise 48

69

Exercise 48 cont.

Exercise 49

CHAPTER TEN

READING MORE DIFFICULT MUSIC

More Complex Rhythms

As mentioned before, the key to keeping correct time in music is knowing how to count the beats of the measure correctly; even with complex times there are simple ways to unravel apparently complicated rhythms.

One of the best ways to do this is through verbal aids, by dividing the beats with a speech pattern that corresponds to the rhythmic pattern. In Chapter Eight we learned to count eighth notes by inserting the word "and" between the main counts. Now we will use the same principle to make accurate counts for sixteenth notes and for combinations of different values.

Most musicians count sixteenth notes like this:

Sixteenth notes

One - e - & - a two - e - & - a three - e - & - a four - e - & - a

A famous teacher once told me, however, that she used the word "caterpillar" as a verbal equivalent in order to establish the rhythm of successive sixteenth notes (the word repeated four times gives the exact rhythm of a ¼ measure of these notes). If this seems bizarre, remember that the very complex and elaborate rhythms of Indian drumming, for example, are passed from father to son in the form of word "poems" that give the exact pattern in speech form.

The "One-e-and-a" method has the advantage of retaining the numbers of the main beats, so that at any moment you know exactly where you are in the measure.

Try the examples below, first counting only, then with a tap of the hand for each note, and finally, when the rhythm is understood, playing each example on the guitar in correct time.

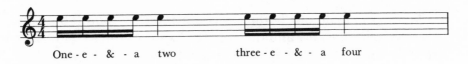

One - e - & - a   two   three - e - & - a   four

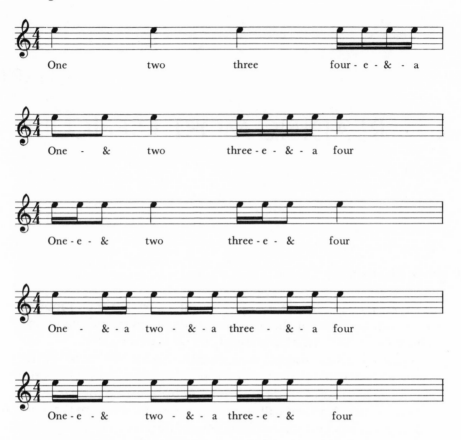

Dotted Notes

The effect of a dot after a note is to increase its value by half again. This has already been seen in connection with the dotted half note:

𝅗𝅥 = two quarter-note counts

𝅗𝅥. = three counts (half as much again)

The dotted quarter note, with a value of three eighth notes or 1½ counts, can be counted by again using the "and" that helped us establish the time of eighth notes. For example, a series of four eighth notes would be counted, "*One*-and-two-and." Since the dotted note is to last for three eighths, it will take up the time of "*one*-and-two":

Many people do not bother to count the first "and," but simply count the first two beats steadily and then use the "and" of the second beat to ensure that the following note starts at the right point:

One   two - &   three   four - &

The familiar tune "Greensleeves" is helpful in establishing the value of the dotted quarter.

three   One   two   three   One   two - &   three   One   two   three   One   two-& three

One   two   three   One   two - &   three   One   two   three   One   two

Now try counting and playing Exercises 50 and 51, with their mixed time values.

Exercise 50

Exercise 51

To count the dotted eighth, which has a value of three sixteenth notes, the "*one*-e-and-a" method may be used.

One - e - & - a   two - e - & - a   three - e - & - a   four - e - & - a

Now try this in the tune given in Exercise 52.

Exercise 52

Triplets

There is one case in which the apparent note values do not seem to add up correctly to the total time of the bar. Sometimes it is desired to break up a beat into three successive notes of equal value and stress; the notes thus grouped are known as a "triplet." The three notes of the triplet are written with a time value as if there were only two.

Consider the following, in $\frac{4}{4}$ time:

This example should be counted, "*One* two three-and-a four," with exactly equal and even stress on each syllable of "three-and-a."

Theoretically, the three notes occupying the space of one quarter-note beat should be called "twelfth notes," since $1/12 \times 3 = 3/12 = \frac{1}{4}$. However, since we have no convenient symbol for a twelfth note it is customary to write the triplet in notes of the next highest value—in this case, eighth notes—indicating that it is a triplet by the figure "3" over the group of notes.

Complex Groups

The triplet principle is applied whenever a group of notes of odd fractional value occupies a beat.

Each of the five notes here has the value of $\frac{1}{20}$ of a $\frac{4}{4}$ measure. Taking the next higher note value, we write the group in sixteenth notes and indicate the pattern with a figure "5" over the group.

Tempo

The time values you have learned above are to enable you to keep the right relationships between notes; but they do not indicate whether a piece is to be played fast or slowly. There is no set length of time for a quarter note, for instance; it must simply occupy one-quarter of the time allotted to a whole note. The speed, or *tempo*, of a piece is indicated in words at the beginning. By custom, Italian words are normally used. The most common, roughly from the slowest to the fastest, convey the following moods:

> *Largo* = Broad, very slow
> *Adagio* = Slow
> *Andante* = Literally, "walking pace"
> *Moderato* = Moderate
> *Allegro* = Cheerful, gay
> *Vivace* = Lively
> *Presto* = Very fast

There are many words used to qualify these main indications; space does not permit us to list all of them, but they can be readily found in any dictionary of musical terms.

Conventional Signs

As well as writing the notes, their timing, and tempo indications, composers also describe in a number of other ways how they wish the music to be played.

A dot place above or below a note means it should be played *staccato*—that is, sharply and quickly. Staccato notes in a sequence sound clearly separated from one another.

The *accent* sign, in contrast, indicates a heavy stress, a "leaning" on the note.

This sign indicates a strong attack, but not sharp and cut off like the staccato.

This indication beside a chord shows that it is to be arpeggiated quickly, the notes sounding almost but not quite simultaneously. It is normal to make this quick arpeggio from the lowest note upward unless otherwise indicated (for instance, by a downward arrow).

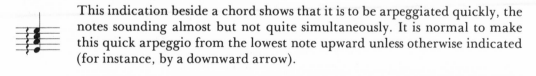

The normal volume indications are *forte* (*f*), meaning loud, and *piano* (*p*), meaning soft. The sign illustrated on top is the *crescendo* sign (literally, "growing"), which indicates a gradual increase in volume. Facing the other way it indicates the opposite, a gradual decrease, and is known as the *diminuendo* sign. The addition of an *m* to an indication (*mf* or *mp*) means moderate loudness or softness, while double letters (*ff*, *pp*, etc.) indicate extreme loudness or softness.

The *fermata*, or hold, sign shown here indicates a pause at this point in the music; the note or rest underneath the fermata should be held.

When a phrase is to be repeated a thick double line is drawn with two dots facing back; this indicates a return to the point where another such sign is shown facing the other way. If there is no other such sign, the repeat is the beginning of the piece.

The letters "D.C." at the end of a piece are short for *da capo* (literally, "from the head"), meaning to play over from the beginning. D.S., short for *dal segno* (literally, "from the sign"), means to play over from a sign most often drawn 𝄋 or ⊕ .

Since notes cannot be written with a time value extending into the next bar, this is accomplished with the tie sign:

This indicates that the note should be held for the combined time value of both the notes tied together, in this case for three counts ("three-four, *one*"). For various reasons the tie is sometimes also used within the bar, where the same rule applies: Play the note once only and hold it for the time value of both.

Positions

Certain signs are used in guitar music to indicate strings, positions, and bars. They are listed here, and will be dealt with in more detail later when you come to learn more of the different positions.

♩②   A number in a circle indicates which string is to be used.

VII   Roman figures normally indicate a bar at the fret number shown. This is sometimes accompanied by the letters C or B—for *capotasto* (It.) or *barré* (Fr.) respectively, meaning "barred."

½VII   This sign indicates a half-bar, sometimes also designated MC (*medio capotasto*).

8th Pos.   This position marking shows the location of the LH on the fingerboard, in this case with the thumb underneath the 8th fret.

The indications for changing position by slide, *portamento*, and so on are best learned in connection with the explanation of these techniques in Chapter Eleven.

Sight-reading

Naturally, considerable practice is necessary in order to achieve familiarity with all the conventional signs of music; there is no better way to do this than to form a habit of daily sight-reading. In doing this it will be helpful to remember the following points:

1. Do not repeat a measure or even a note that you have played correctly, but keep moving forward. The repeated note achieves nothing, and divides the concentration, which should be focused entirely on what is to come.

2. Read the complete piece—or that part of it set aside for the day's reading—from beginning to end, not piecemeal. This is a study habit which should be formed at the beginning; it will help you greatly in subsequent reading and memorization.

3. Avoid trying to read pieces that are too difficult technically, however keen you may be to play them. You will go too slowly, and possibly give up after a few bars. The essential thing is to try to match your reading to your technical progress.

Mastering What You Have Learned

In general, few elements of music present as great a problem as does keeping correct time. If you run into difficulties here, remember that any person with musical training can help you, as the rules are not confined to guitar. It is most important to master the rules of notation through considerable practice at this stage before continuing to the next chapters, with their more advanced techniques and musical illustrations. For this reason you should refer to the list of recommended music in Appendix 3 at the back of this book, in addition to the following practice pieces.

In Classical Style

Frederick Noad

This is fairly straightforward reading, but start slowly so that you are not rushed in measure 4. In measure 10, let the lower part "answer" the quarter notes of the previous measure with firm thumb strokes; do this also in measure 12.

Remember to pull off smoothly for the descending *ligados*, but avoid just lifting the finger.

It is most important to read the fingering correctly from the first, as it makes the piece easier to play.

Popular Air

Anonymous
Arr. Frederick Noad

At the beginning of the nineteenth century a number of tunes achieved particular popularity with the pioneers of the six-string guitar, as evidenced by the number of surviving arrangements. This tune was sung to the lyric "My Lodging It Is on the Cold Ground," although today it is better known as "Believe Me If All Those Endearing Young Charms."

Carnavalitos

Peruvian Folk Dance
Arr. Frederick Noad

This typical dance from Peru is fun to play and technically easy. It is important to pay attention to accent and stress signs to achieve the typical rhythm. The two arpeggiated final chords should be played with the fleshy part of the thumb and immediately damped (see Chapter Five).

Moorish Dance

Spanish Traditional
Arr. Frederick Noad

Most flamenco players have in their repertoire some form of Moorish dance, this being handed down from the time when the Moors occupied Spain. This piece should be played at a moderate speed. Feel the heavy two-beat rhythm. Remember to alternate the RH fingers when you come to the repeated notes. The *ligados* at the beginning and end of the piece are good practice for the deliberate hammerstroke. The mood should be dramatic and mysterious.

Jesu, Joy of Man's Desiring

Johann Sebastian Bach (1685–1750)
Arr. Frederick Noad

This beautiful theme introduces here the use of the low D obtained by tuning the 6th string down a tone. To tune, lower the 6th string until it sounds a perfect octave with the open 4th string. The notes will now be as shown.

This D tuning is quite common. The piece should be played at a steady pace, using free strokes with both fingers and thumb.

6th in D

D	E	F	F#	G
open	2nd fret	3rd fret	4th fret	5th fret

6th to D

Lilliburlero

Irish Folk Song
Arr. Frederick Noad

This old Irish folk tune should sound lively and gay. In the 2nd measure, try to ease into the barred position without "grabbing" at it, and remember to count the dotted notes correctly. In the 13th measure, place the bar *before* playing the F♯. Use rest strokes where possible to bring out the melody.

Sevillanas

Arr. Frederick Noad

This Spanish dance should be played in strict tempo. The first part imitates the characteristic *rasgueado* (which you will learn in later chapters). Measures 4–6 indicate to the dancers the tune that is to follow, and they commence dancing at measure 7. The *copla*, or main song (literally, "lyric"), is played three times, and to be strictly correct should end the third time through on the first beat of the final

measure with a sharp stroke of the fingernails to sound an E chord which is immediately damped, instead of the four sixteenth notes and quarter note played the first two times through. This is a typical *sevillanas* tune, of which there are many in various keys but always following the same general structure.

All the melodic parts should be played with strong rest strokes.

CHAPTER ELEVEN

LEARNING THE FINGERBOARD

You will have noticed by this point that, although many accompaniments and simple tunes can be played in the first position, advanced players tend to use the whole range of the guitar, and that most solo works of musical value entail the use of more positions.

Assuming that you are by now able to read, though perhaps slowly, in the first position, it is time to tackle the higher reaches of the fingerboard. It is clearly impossible to read advanced studies unless the notes of the fingerboard have been thoroughly memorized. The purpose of this chapter is to make this task as easy as possible.

Learning Notes Across the Frets

Just as in learning the staff it is easier to learn the notes by lines and then by spaces, rather than in alphabetical succession, so is it easier to learn the guitar fingerboard by memorizing the notes across a given fret, then across the others. It is of little value, for example, to take one string at a time and finger the frets, saying to yourself "E, F, F♯, G, G♯, A"; by now you know the order of the notes anyway, and could easily just repeat them without really associating them with the correct fret. It is of much greater value to take, for instance, the 7th fret, playing the notes and repeating their names to yourself as shown here.

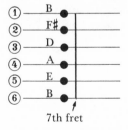

It would be of great help to at the same time jot down the notes of that fret on a piece of manuscript paper, so that you can keep clearly in mind which B or E you are learning.

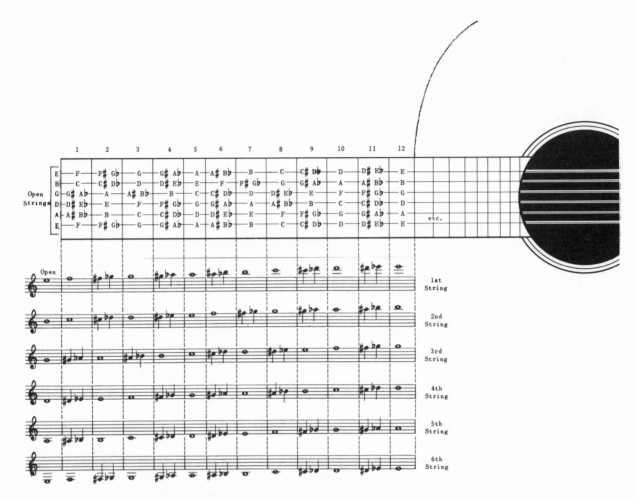

Figure 26. Complete Notes to the Twelfth Fret

Learning the fingerboard certainly involves work, but you will be amazed at the results if you approach the task methodically. Conversely, you will find reading unbearably laborious if you have only a hazy notion of where the notes are on the fingerboard. Figure 26 gives a complete diagram of the notes on the first twelve frets.

Equivalent Notes

Some beginners are disturbed by the fact that the same musical note at the same pitch can be found at different points and on different strings of the guitar. In fact, this is a great advantage, for two reasons: first, because each string has a characteristic tonal quality and thus the possibility of playing the same notes in different positions adds to the variety of tone color and contrast available; second, because it is thus often possible to stay in position on the fingerboard instead of jumping back and forth for the various notes.

Equivalent notes can also be used as an aid to memorizing the fingerboard. It is a good idea, for example, to learn first where all the equivalents to the open strings are, up to the 12th fret (diagrammed in Figure 27).

When a note is written for guitar in a position other than the first, it is customary to write the string number beside it in a circle, unless the string or position is obvious.

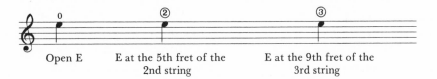

Open E E at the 5th fret of the E at the 9th fret of the
       2nd string   3rd string

After learning the equivalents to the open strings, it would be good practice to find for yourself the equivalents to other notes, and for this the following rule will help you.

The Rule of Five

With one exception, the equivalent note for any you choose can be found on the string below by adding five to the fret number. For example, F on the 1st string is found at the 1st fret. Its equivalent on the next string, the 2nd string, is found by adding five to the first number: 5 + 1 = 6. Therefore the 6th fret on the 2nd string will also be F. The exception occurs when finding a 3rd-string equivalent to a 2nd-string note: Between these two strings only, add four to the

Figure 27. Equivalent Notes

first number. For example, the 3rd fret of the 2nd string is D. The same note on the 3rd string is at the 7th fret (3 + 4).

Whether you use equivalent notes as a memory aid, learn them across the frets one by one, or do both, the important thing to realize is that an effort of memorization is necessary. Just trying to read music in higher positions is not sufficient, since progress this way tends to be slow and tedious.

It is the combination of learning notes by rote and sight-reading to reinforce this that will produce the best results. In addition, it is not necessary to always have a guitar at hand in order to work on memorizing the fingerboard; otherwise wasted time, such as that spent waiting for a bus, may be used to recapitulate the positions of the notes and visualize how they look in notation. Remember that, whatever field of guitar music interests you, you cannot say you know your instrument until you become thoroughly familiar with the notes on it.

Exercises 53 and 54 give practice in the equivalent-note approach by each showing a melody in three different positions on th fingerboard.

Exercise 53

(a) 1st Position

(b) 5th Position

(c) 9th Position

Exercise 54

(a) 2nd Position

(b) 4th Position

(c) 9th Position

Changing Position

To preserve the flow of a piece of music it is naturally desirable to make the LH position changes as smooth as possible; to assist you in this, special techniques are available.

The simplest position change occurs when an intervening open-string note allows the complete removal of the left hand.

In this example the LH can locate the F on the 2nd string while the open E is still sounding.

Usually, however, an open string is not available, and one of the following methods is used.

The Guide Finger

In this case a finger on a string is moved up the same string to the new position, thus guiding the hand.

Note that here the finger simply uses the string as a "guide rail," and should not sound as it makes the movement. For this reason it is raised slightly from the fingerboard as it moves, but still keeps contact with the string. This is shown by the notation −1, −2, −3 or −4, depending on which finger is the guide.

The finger used as a guide need not necessarily be the last played before the change, but may have been left in place in preparation for it. In this example the 1st finger is left on after playing the C in preparation for its move up the string to the E.

Changing position downward follows the same principle: Here the 3rd finger guides the hand from the 3rd to the 1st position:

Exercises 55 and 56 afford an opportunity to practice these position changes.

Exercise 55

Exercise 56

Portamento

In contrast to the guide-finger change of position, which aims at a silent move, the *portamento* deliberately sounds the varying pitch as the finger slides from a note in one position to another. The effect is graceful, adding a *legato*, or smooth, feeling to a melody. To execute the portamento do the following:

1. Play the first note with the RH. Hold it for its full value.
2. Then very quickly move to the second note by sliding up the string while maintaining pressure on it.
3. Play the second note with the RH the moment the finger is established in the new position.

Note that in this example the E is only played *once*; the small note is simply a conventional indication of a portamento, and distinguishes it from a *slide* (see below).

Sometimes another finger plays the second note. Here the 1st finger moves only as far as the 4th fret, leaving the hand in correct position for the 2nd finger to play the E. As before the E is played only once.

These shifts can be practiced in Exercise 57.

Exercise 57

Exercise 57 cont.

The Slide

The slide resembles the portamento, except that the second note is not played by the RH but sounded by the force of the slide itself.

In this example the C is played by the right hand; then the 1st finger slides rapidly and firmly to sound the D, which is *not* played by the RH. As with the portamento, it is important to hold the first note for its full time value and then move with speed and precision to the second.

Both the slide and portamento can be practiced in Exercise 58.

Exercise 58

Mastering What You Have Learned

Knowledge of the fingerboard, and the ability to move smoothly on it from position to position, will open up for you a new field of playing, including new sounds and tonal contrasts. Your left hand will develop in strength and ability, and you will be on the way to the more advanced playing discussed in the following chapters. Considerable practice is necessary at this point, for learning the fingerboard certainly takes time. It will be time well spent.

The following pieces provide a pleasant way to practice.

Arpeggio Study

Frederick Noad

This study uses the third position, but should present no difficulty providing that careful attention is paid to the fingering. It should be played at a leisurely speed and not be rushed. As explained on page 76, D.C. means "from the beginning"; *al fine* means "to the point marked *fine* (or finish)."

Minuet

Frederick Noad

This piece is written in the style of a simple Baroque minuet. It should be played at a comfortable speed, with extra emphasis on the first beat of each measure to accentuate the dance rhythm. The first time through, at the end of the first half, play the measure marked 1, which leads back to the beginning. The second time omit that measure, play the one marked 2, and continue.

Españoleta

Gaspar Sanz (17th Century)

For the purposes of this book I have omitted ornamentation (mordents, trills, etc.), which I feel adds unneccessary difficulty at this point and could possibly put a beautiful and otherwise straight-forward piece out of range.

With the first themes here bring out the melody strongly with rest strokes. The eighth-note variations should not be rushed, and the original themes should be kept firmly in mind, slightly extra emphasis being given to the first beat of the measure in this section.

The last four measures should be played not mechanically but majestically, with a gradual slowing down to the final chord.

Gaspar Sanz

Air

*Giovanni Battista Pergolesi
(1710–1736)*

This piece is a solo arrangement of the song "Que Ne Suis-je La Fougere." The feeling is romantic, and the tempo should be moderate and flowing. The stretch at seems awkward at first, but will come with practice. In spite of the repeat sign at the beginning of the third line the music should flow from the previous measure with no break in rhythm.

Muss I Denn

German Folk Song
Arr. Frederick Noad

This piece is arranged from a famous German folk song. It is intended for the practice of thirds (intervals embracing three diatonic degrees), and briefly intro- duces the fifth position. As always, try to make the LH glide, rather than jump, between positions.

99

Mañanitas

Mexican Folk Song
Arr. Frederick Noad

This famous Mexican Christmas song serves to introduce the higher reaches of the guitar and also to provide practice in handling sixths (intervals embracing six diatonic degrees) and thirds. The upper part should be made to sing, and the tempo should be moderate and not too strict.

Romance

Frederick Noad

The key of E minor is always a favorite with guitarists, since it sems to have a particular haunting quality. This little romance should present no particular difficulty once the positions are worked out. Read the piece through completely several times before attempting to memorize it.

Ballet

Anonymous
Arr. Frederick Noad

This dance tune comes from a large collection compiled by the German musician and theorist Michael Praetorius (1571-1621). The tunes include some of the most popular of the time, this, one of the best of them, sounds well on the guitar. No particular instruments are specified in the original versions.

Prelude

Frederick M. Noad

This prelude is mainly intended as a more advanced study in the hammer-stroke. The triplet groups should be played deliberately, taking particular care not to hurry them. Observe also the effect of open strings against a higher note on a lower string. The tempo should be somewhat slower than *andante*, with a free lyrical approach.

In the fourth measure before the end be careful to damp the open A so that it does not sound against the open B in the following measure.

Prelude

Frédéric Chopin (1810–1849)
Arr. Frederick Noad

This little prelude has long been a favorite with guitarists; it is not too difficult, although it touches the fourteenth position! It should be played slowly and peacefully, making the notes sing. One of the advantages of the guitar is that it can produce more tonal variety than the piano, for which this piece was originally written.

Allegretto

Fernando Sor (1778–1839)

Sor, one of the best-known composers for guitar in the Classical period, was one of the first to introduce it to the concert hall. This lighthearted piece is not difficult, although it explores the fingerboard's higher reaches. Play the grace notes (small notes with a line through them—see A) very fast; they have no time value but simply "borrow" from the note they precede. Play the note formed by the first finger and then immediately hammer down the second finger to play the succeeding note.

Linden Lea

*Ralph Vaughan Williams
(1872–1958)
Arr. Frederick Noad*

This arrangement from a composition by Ralph Vaughan Williams should be played lyrically and freely once it is mastered. It is intended as practice for changing smoothly to the third position and for learning that position.

Although the three parts call for the use of free strokes, the melody should be emphasized as much as possible; slight arpeggiation of the chords will sometimes help to achieve this. By playing the notes of a chord successively from lowest to highest it becomes possible to give an extra "lift" to the melody note.

CHAPTER TWELVE

COLORFUL ACCOMPANIMENTS

Many songs can be accompanied simply by strumming a few chords in first position and indeed there are many that sound better with a simple accompaniment than an elaborate one. It is also true, however, that most professional singer-players tend to use the full scope of the guitar to produce colorful accompaniment.

As an example, the reader is recommended to listen with a critical ear to the different approaches of such folk players as Theodore Bikel, Judy Collins, Bob Dylan, Joan Baez, Leonard Cohen, and Pete Seeger, to mention only a few.

Special Effects

First let us consider some of the "special effects" of the guitar.

Natural Harmonics

Harmonics, or bell tones, can be produced by touching a string lightly with the appropriate LH finger at certain frets without depressing the string, and then taking the finger away the minute the string has been sounded by the RH.

The easiest harmonics to sound are to be found at the 12th fret. As an example, follow these steps:

1. With the little finger of the LH, touch the 4th string lightly at the 12th fret.
2. With the RH thumb, play a rest stroke on the 4th string.
3. As the RH thumb completes its stroke, remove the LH finger to allow the string to vibrate freely. The bell-like tone should continue to sound.

When you can sound this harmonic satisfactorily try the other strings at the 12th fret.

Harmonics can also be obtained at the 7th and 5th frets, but these are weaker and more difficult to sound, so it is better to master the technique first at the 12th fret. Weaker harmonics can be found at other points on the guitar, but these are rarely used.

Octave Harmonics

A harmonic can be obtained an octave (twelve frets) above any note, including those fretted by the LH. However, since in the latter case the LH is needed to fret the note it is necessary to use the RH to both lightly touch the string and pluck it. This is achieved by touching with the *i* finger and plucking with the *a* finger. As an example, follow these steps (see also Figure 28):

1. With the LH 1st finger, fret F on the 1st fret of the string.
2. With the RH *i* finger, lightly touch the 1st string over the 13th fret, without depressing the string.
3. Pluck the string with the *a* finger, removing the whole hand as the stroke is completed.

Do not worry if you have difficulty at first; this is a difficult technique and takes considerable practice. Most important is to remember that the touch by the *i* finger must always be twelve frets above the note fretted by the LH.

Figure 28. Octave Harmonics

The Snare-Drum Effect

A surprisingly realistic snare-drum sound can be achieved by the following procedure (refer to Figure 29).

1. With the RH, pull the 5th string over the 6th at the 9th fret.

2. Then, with the LH, pin them down so that they are held crossed at the 9th fret.
3. With the RH, pull sharply across the two strings, using the fingernails and alternating fingers to achieve the rhythm desired.

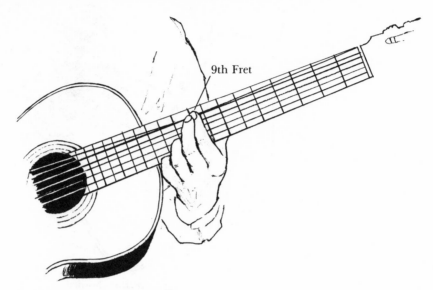

9th Fret

Figure 29. Snare-Drum Effect

Tambor

The dramatic effect of the *tambor* (Spanish—literally "drum") can be obtained by fingering a full chord with the LH and, instead of plucking the strings, tapping on the bridge with the side of the thumb. The RH should be very loose, allowing the thumb to bounce off after tapping the bridge. The best position is right over the bridge bone, as illustrated in Figure 30. The best effect comes with chords that use many open strings, as for instance E minor. Remember that the tap will sound all the strings, so a chord involving only four or five strings is not suitable.

Vibrato

The tone of a note can be much enhanced, and its duration seemingly extended, by the use of vibrato in the LH. There are two methods of producing this effect. The first, lengthwise vibrato, is achieved by vibrating the LH from left to right along the line of the fingerboard, without lessening the pressure from the finger fretting the note. The second method consists of pulling the string sideways back and forth across the fingerboard with the LH finger for a short distance, at the same rate of vibration as in the first method.

The effect of both forms of vibrato is to minutely raise and lower the pitch of the note, producing an undulating or wavering sound which is very beautiful when done correctly.

A general rule—intended only as a guide and not invariable—is as follows:

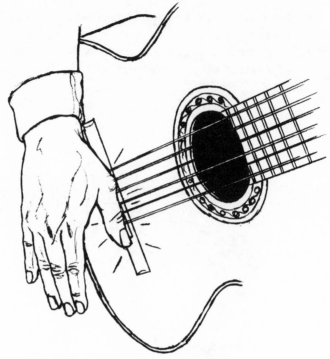

Strings may be played open or chorded.

Figure 30. Tambor Effect

1. When fretting the notes of the first four frets, use the sideways vibrato since the lengthwise method is weaker in these positions.
2. From the 5th to the 12th fret the lengthwise vibrato is the most satisfactory.
3. Above the 12th fret it may be necessary to use the sideways vibrato again, as the other is not practicable in the high positions.

In the opinion of the author, the sideways vibrato should be used with caution, since too violent a pull to the side results in an extreme change of pitch which, although sometimes suitable in the blues and similar styles (see p. 118 below), is excessive elsewhere.

The Rasgueado

The *rasgueado* (Spanish for "strumming," literally) is widely used in Spanish music, and when used in accompaniment always adds a Spanish flavor. Essentially, it is nothing more than a scrape across the strings with the nails of the RH, but extremely complex rhythms can be achieved by its use in conjunction with up and down strokes of the 1st finger or entire hand.

Figure 31 shows the preparation, execution, and completion of the *rasgueado*. Here are the movements in stages:

1. Finger an A chord with the LH. With the RH, place the thumb in a position of support on the 6th string.
2. Curl the fingers of the RH up into the palm.

Figure 31. The *Rasgueado*
  (A) The fingers are curled and ready to start the *rasgueado*.
  (B) The *i* and *o* fingers play, and are followed down by the *m* finger.
  (C) The *i* finger plays last, completing the movement.

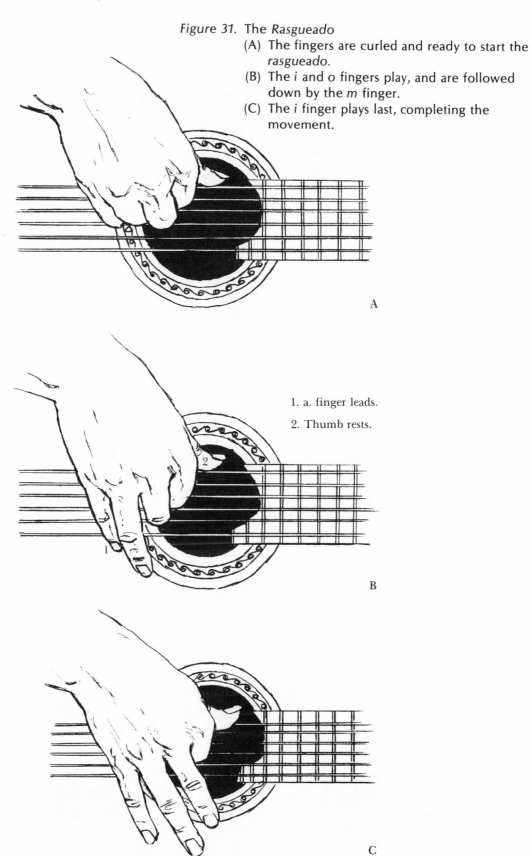

A

1. a. finger leads.

2. Thumb rests.

B

C

3. Leading with the little finger, scrape the backs of the fingernails successively across the strings, leaving each finger curled up until its turn comes to play. (One can also lead with the *a* finger.)

The greatest difficulty in learning the *rasgueado* lies in making the fingers sufficiently separate so that they strike the strings in succession. Failure here results in a short, indistinct sound, whereas the well-executed *rasgueado* should be a roll containing four distinct sounds as each finger crosses the strings. Particular difficulty lies in separating the *a* finger and the *m* finger, which have a tendency to remain together. To improve this situation, it is a good idea to practice the *rasgueado* without the little finger (a form also widely used), making the *a* finger lead.

In conjunction with the *rasgueado* two strokes are widely used: a downstroke across the strings from 6th to 1st string, performed with the back of the nail of the *i* finger; and the corresponding upstroke from 1st to 6th string, achieved by pulling the *i* finger back across the strings. Sometimes, for emphasis, the downstroke is made with the nails of the *i, m,* and *a* fingers together; note that the purpose here is to make a single sound, not a *rasgueado*.

Until these strokes are mastered, it is a good idea to leave the thumb resting on the 6th string as support for the RH, and concentrate on striking the other five.

Because of the complications in writing *rasgueados* in standard musical notation, it is customary to employ special symbols, placed above the staff. Although not universal, the following are widely used:

↓ Downstroke (6th to 1st string)

↑ Upstroke (1st to 6th string)

⦚ *Rasgueado*

⦚ ↑ *Rasgueado* followed by immediate upstroke, performed as one movement.

When these symbols are associated with standard notation they may be "stretched" sideways to show the notes covered, as in the following examples, which show respectively a *rasgueado* that is all downstrokes and a *rasgueado* followed by an upstroke.

Sometimes the chords are written in full, but often just the chord symbols are used, as in the example below—a well-known rhythm from Malaga. In this example full barred chords should be used.

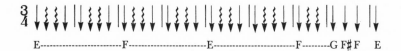

E------------------------F----------------------E---------------------F--------G F♯ F   E

In standard notation this rhythm would be written thus (the letter "l" is used here for the little finger):

i   l a m i   l a m i   i   i   l a m i   l a m i   i

In a word-rhythm this would be "*Pom*-tiddley-pom-tiddley-pom-pom, *pom*-tiddley-pom-tiddley-pom-pom," etc.

Standard notation for the *rasgueado* is often abbreviated, too, as shown here:

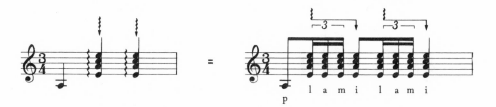

A useful pattern for the accompaniment of many Latin American songs includes a simple *rasgueado*:

i   l a m i   i   i   i   i   l a m i   i   i   i

As in the *Malagueña* (rhythm from Malaga) above, the *rasgueado* here starts with the little finger on the first note of the sixteenth-note triplet and finishes with the index finger on the following eighth note. The word-rhythm is "*pom*-tiddley-pom-pom-pom-pom, *pom*-tiddley-pom-pom-pom-pom," etc. For a complete song to this pattern see "Coplas," on p. 171 in Appendix 1.

More about the *rasgueado* is included in Chapter Fifteen, "Playing Flamenco Music."

The Golpe

The "golpe" is a Spanish term applied to the rhythmic tap on the guitar used widely in flamenco to acentuate or complete the rhythm. The guitar is struck sharply, usually with the *a* finger, at a point beyond the 1st string. Flamenco guitars are provided with a protective plate in this area (see Figure 4, p. 9) to avoid damage to the top. If your guitar is not so protected, the *golpe* should be used sparingly, and then only on the harder wood of the bridge. In flamenco, the *golpe* is used both by itself and with a simultaneous *i* finger downstroke which it often serves to emphasize.

The *golpe* is indicated in music by a cross:

A Mexican variant. In Mexico and elsewhere in Latin America a type of *golpe* is used whereby the strings are struck by the RH at a point just beyond the soundhole and above the end of the fingerboard. This produces a percussive slapping sound as the strings strike the frets, and is used effectively for rhythmic accentuation. For a very marked effect the flat of the hand may be used; otherwise, use the side of the thumb, which has the advantage of less displacement of the hand. A good example is afforded by the *Huapango* rhythm:

To play this example, first prepare the A minor chord with the left hand. Then make two distinct taps with the side of the thumb across the 4th, 5th, and 6th strings before sweeping down and back with the thumb. When the thumb strikes the fingerboard it is at about 45° angle to the frets.

Pizzicato

When violinists pluck the strings of their instruments instead of bowing, the effect is known as "pizzicato." This is imitated on the guitar by muffling the strings at the bridge with the side of the RH, the notes being played with the thumb. The muted effect thus obtained affords a marked contrast in tone color to the normal sound of the guitar.

Figure 32 shows the RH position for pizzicato. The side of the RH should rest just behind the bridge bone—i.e., the opposide side to the soundhole—where the degree of muting can be controlled.

Pizzicato is normally indicated in notation by the abbreviation "pizz.," and the notes concerned are marked staccato. (Sometimes a line is drawn above the staff to show the exact duration of the pizzicato passage.)

pizz.

Hand rests gently just before the bridge bone.

Figure 32. Pizzicato

Tremolo

The effect of a continuous melody can be produced on the guitar by the fast repetition of each note. In the most usual pattern the thumb plays as in an arpeggio pattern, each thumb note being followed by a melody note repeated three times.

The general principles are the same as for arpeggio playing, and it is good practice to place both thumb and *a* finger before playing each group. This assists particularly when the tremolo takes place on inside strings. The technique should be practiced until absolute evenness is obtained; a practical example of it is given at the end of Chapter Fourteen with the time-honored melody "Greensleeves."

National and Regional Characteristics

Part of the art of song accompaniment is to suit the guitar part to the song's national or regional origins and its period in history. The beautiful lute songs of the Elizabethan period, for instance, are best accompanied by the nearest possible imitation of the original lute arrangements, which are rich in counter-melodies, cross-rhythms, and harmonic variety. On the other hand, many-versed narrative songs that relate a dramatic story are usually better supported by a simple chord pattern, since an exact and elaborate accompaniment can become irritating when repeated over and over for a multitude of short verses. The blues, work songs, and so on from the black American heritage require the traditionally strong and characteristic rhythm, while Spanish and South American songs often call for typical percussive and strumming effects.

It is beyond the scope of this book to deal with all these in detail, as space permits the citing of only a few examples. Ultimately your ear will train you better than can written music; the greatest benefit can be obtained by listening carefully and analytically to performances, "live" or on records, of recognized artists.

The following section presents pieces that are complete examples of accompaniment in five widely contrasting styles. These are but a few of the many available, of course, but by studying these carefully you will at least be on the way to using your guitar imaginatively and with a variety of styles.

Blues

A chord sequence for the twelve-bar blues was given in Chapter Seven (p. 49), and a simple strum on these chords would be sufficient accompaniment if you are merely providing a "rhythm section" for other instruments. However, for the solo song with a guitar it is customary to provide more elaborate patterns, usually involving syncopation.

Syncopation. A melody whose notes fall on normally unaccented parts of the measure is one cause of the effect of syncopation.

In this example the melody notes occur on the second half of each beat—normally weak—while the bass notes occur on the beat.

If instead of the second half of the beat for the melody we choose the fourth quarter of it, the effect is even more pronounced.

To establish the dotted eighth and sixteenth note pattern we can use the "*one*-e-and-a" technique. However, when it becomes familiar it would be sufficient omitting the "e-and" part, to just count, "*One*--a, *two*--a, *three*--a, *four*--a."

Play these examples several times until you feel and understand the syncopated effect.

Applying the principle now to a blues accompaniment, we may keep the chords on the beat and provide syncopation with melody notes:

Sometimes the bass line has the sixteenth note usually when the melody note is held. The following is typical mixed movement between melody and bass:

A very popular figure is one with a typical Tar*rump*titum pattern. Here the dotted-eighth-sixteenth combination alternates between treble and bass, with the middle voices keeping the steady rhythm. This is a good pattern for experimentation with a variety of chords, since it has a very typical and authentic feeling.

You will notice that in all the previous examples something has happened *on* the beat, thus helping to accentuate the syncopated effect of the offbeat notes. This is not always done, however, and in such cases a strong sense of the rhythm must be kept by the performer, perhaps with a tap of the foot at first.

For instance, the final measure of the twelve often ends as in this example (accent marks show where the foot tap would fall).

I suggest a thorough study of this syncopation section to be sure that the rhythms are understood and felt, before trying to read the complete blues accompaniment ("Blues") below.

Blues vibrato or "bending the note." An extreme form of vibrato can be produced by pulling the string sideways with the LH finger holding the note after it is played by the RH. In the blues this is usually done quite slowly, producing a noticeable increase in pitch as the string is pulled which then diminishes as it returns to the central position. The LH finger remains in contact with string and fingerboard. The number of times the string is "bent" and returned depends on the value of the note concerned.

Blues

Traditional
Arr. Frederick Noad

A complete blues accompaniment involves a certain dialogue between voice and guitar. Here the guitar begins with an introductory four bars that are equivalent in harmony to the last four of a twelve bar sequence. When the voice enters the accompaniment becomes mainly chordal, until the voice pauses, when the guitar customarily offers some melody or variation to the the "space." Then when the voice returns the guitar resumes its straightforward chording.

Calypso

The most typical rhythm in Calypso style consists of eight equal eighth-note beats stressed thus: *one*-two-three, *one*-*two*-three, *one*-two. Written in $\frac{8}{8}$ time it has this form:

This can be expressed in simple arpeggio forms, which for the gentler type of song can be most effective.

However, for the heartier versions, such as the piece below—"Sloop John B."—a full chord pattern is typical and most enjoyable to play when mastered. Here are the movements for this type of pattern on the E major chord:

1. Having fingered the E chord with the LH, play a strong downstroke with the RH *i* finger, following it with the thumb, which plays a weaker downstroke; complete this movement by pulling back the *i* finger in an upstroke, also weak. The time of these movements is even, but is stressed thus: *one*-two-three.

2. The next step consists of playing the same three strokes, but this time giving more weight to the thumb stroke to increase the accent. The stress here should be as follows: *one*-*two*-three—*two*" being the heavy thumb stroke.

3. The final movement is an even down–up stroke with the *i* finger, giving slightly more weight to the downstroke.

In notation the whole pattern looks like this:

Practice the beat until it is automatic, before attempting to sing the melody to it; otherwise the results are likely to be less than coordinated.

The Sloop John B.

Traditional
Arr. Frederick Noad

We come on the sloop John B. My grand - fa - ther and me, A -

round Nas - sau town we did roam. Drink-in' all

night, Got in-to a fight. Well, I

The Sloop John B. cont.

feel   so break - up   I want to go   home.

Chorus:
So hoist up the John B. sails,

See how the mainsail sets,

Send for the captain ashore, let me go home,

Let me go home, I want to go home,

Well I feel so break-up

I want to go home.

2. The first mate he got drunk,

Broke up the captain's trunk.

Constable had to come and take him away.

Sheriff John Stone, please let me alone,

I feel so break-up

I want to go home.

Chorus:
So hoist up, *etc.*

3. The poor cook he got the fits

And threw away all of my grits,

Then he took and he drank up all of my corn.

Let me go home, Why don't you let me go home?

This is the worst trip

Since I was born.

Chorus

Spanish Folk Music: *La Petenera*

In Spain the contrasting rhythm of $\frac{6}{8}$ alternating with $\frac{3}{4}$ has been popular for centuries, and an understanding of this curiosity is most helpful in the exploration of Spanish music.

$\frac{6}{8}$ time is considered as two triplets, and counted with a stress on "one" and "four."

One two three *four* five six   *One* two three *four* five six

In $\frac{3}{4}$ time, as we have seen, there is a stress on the first beat, as in waltz time.

Both time signatures involve the same amount of time, (six eighth notes per measure = three quarter notes); the difference lies in the stress. When put together in sequence, they are counted thus:

One two three *four* five six   *One* & two & three &

The "ands" are inserted in the $\frac{3}{4}$ measure as a counting aid which may be abandoned when the relationship is understood. For now it is important to realize that the length of the eighth note and of the complete measure does not vary: an even tap will coincide with each of the number and the "and" counts.

La Petenera

Spanish Traditional
Arr. Frederick Noad

In the accompaniment pattern the bass notes are played with the RH thumb, the chords in the 6/8 measures with an *i* finger downstroke, and the *rasgueados* in the 3/4 bars with all four fingers. Since the last finger (*i*) to play coincides with the beat, the *rasgueado* must start slightly before it. (Refer back to p. 113 for an explanation of the *rasgueado* notation in 3/4 bars here.)

oy-es dob-lar la cam - pa-na, No pre - gun - te Quien ha muer-to,

Por - que a ti   te lo di - ran,   Por - que a ti   te lo di -

ran,   "Tu   mis - mo   Re - mor - di - mien - to,"   Si

oy - es dob - lar la cam - pa - na No pre - gun - te Quien ha muer - to

La Bamba

Mexican Folk Song
Arr. Frederick Noad

From the region of Veracruz on the Gulf Coast of Mexico comes this exuberant and popular party song. Music groups of the area use the harp as well as guitar; hence the arpeggiated introduction here, which may be repeated *ad libitum* until the singer is ready to start. The chords may be played either with a single finger back and forth or, where volume is needed, by the *i*, *m*, and *a* fingers joined together. As before, practice the accompaniment pattern until it becomes automatic.

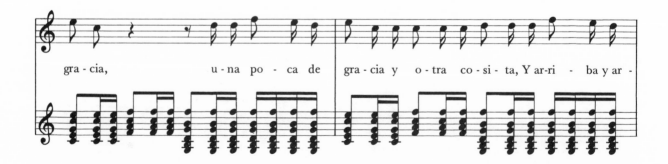

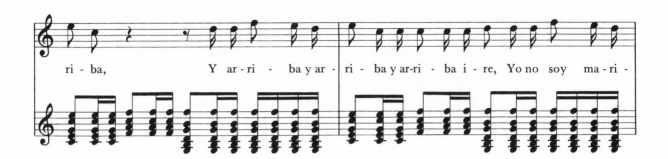

ri - ba,   Y ar - ri - ba y ar - ri - ba y ar - ri - ba i - re, Yo no soy ma - ri -

ne - ro,   Yo no soy ma - ri - ne - ro, por ti se - re por ti se - re por ti se - re.

2. Aunque soy chiquitito, aunque soy chiquitito de inspiración,
   Me encanto la Bamba, me encanto la Bamba de corazón,
   Y arriba, y arriba, *etc.*

3. Esos que no me quieren, esos que no me quieren porque no tengo
   La nariz apilada, la nariz apilada y los ojos negros,
   Y arriba, y arriba, *etc.*

4. Ay te pido, te pido, Ay te pido, te pido de compasión,
   Que se acabe la Bamba, que se acabe la Bamba ven otro son,
   Y arriba, y arriba, *etc.*

Awake Sweet Love

John Dowland (1562–1626)
Transcribed by Frederick Noad
Poet Unknown

In contrast to the preceding folk music this Elizabethan song was typically written to be accompanied by the lute. Notice that, although simple, the accompaniment is almost a solo in itself, its melodies making a fine contrast to the voice.

The lute is similar in many ways to the guitar, although of different ancestry; the music written for it, buried for many generations in obscurity, is now a fertile source for guitarists.

A - wake, sweet love, Thou art re - turned:
Let love, which ne - ver ab - sent dies,

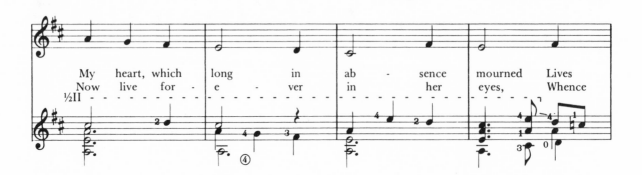

My heart, which long in ab - sence mourned Lives
Now live for - e - ver in her eyes, Whence

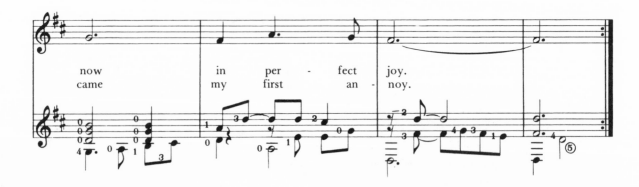

now in per - fect joy.
came my first an - noy.

128

Colorful Accompaniments

On - ly her - self hath seem - ed fair: She on - ly
De - spair did make me wish to die; That I my

I could love, She on - ly drove
joys might end: She on - ly, which

me to de - spair, When she un - kind did prove.
did make me fly, My state may now a - mend.

2. If she esteem thee now aught worth,
   She will not grieve thy love henceforth,
   Which so despair hath proved.
   Despair hath provèd now in me,
   That love will not unconstant be,
   Though long in vain I loved.
   If she at last reward thy love,

And all thy harms repair,
Thy happiness will sweeter prove,
Raised up from deep despair.
And if that now thou welcome be,
When thou with her dost meet,
She all this while but played with thee,
To make thy joys more sweet.

CHAPTER THIRTEEN

FINGER-PICKING

The name "finger-picking" is given to a particular style of accompaniment, also used for solos, in which the thumb establishes a firm and regular rhythm against which the *i* or *m* finger plays a melodic part. The offbeat or syncopated effects here are often quite striking, and the impression is sometimes given of two instruments playing, due to the independent rhythm established by the thumb.

The principle is probably most easily demonstrated by taking some chords and constructing an accompaniment in fingerpicking style. For instance, with the C major chord a typical thumb pattern would be this:

After practicing this, the other notes of the C chord may be added.

The effect of two musical lines is given by accenting and holding the E's to give the following result:

However, the simpler form of notation for this is easier to read and therefore more commonly used.

130

Related chords in the key of C would be fingered as follows:

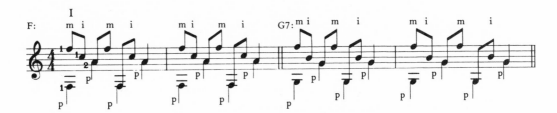

It should be emphasized that, as with all accompaniments, the use of a single pattern without variation can quickly become monotonous. Variety can be achieved by switching patterns, pausing for a measure or so, introducing variety by using *ligado* technique, changing bass notes, and so on. These methods can better be understood if you play through the practical examples that follow.

Alternative Patterns

In these instances the initial simple pattern is varied slightly for increased rhythmic effect where appropriate.

The bass pattern can be increased to include the octave:

In addition it can be moved stepwise for variety from the fixed pattern, as in this transition from G to G7.

Often — depending on the melody to be accompanied — the highest note of the combination can be varied for additional interest.

Both upward and downward *ligados* can be added, and are quite typical of the style. These are simple examples:

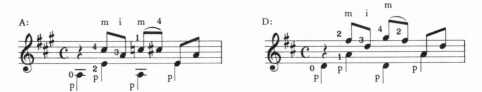

Obviously it is impossible to give all varieties of pattern that go to make up this style of playing, particularly as this should be a field for individal invention and experimentation. The main point to remember is the fixed and steady rhythm maintained by the thumb.

For practice purposes three songs arranged in finger-picking style — "Careless Love," "Poor Boy," and "Banks of the Ohio" — can be found in Appendix 1 at the end of this book; and for an easy example of a solo in this form, a version of "Silver Sand Rag" follows.

For further study of this style, the best plan is to listen carefully to performances by such trendsetters as Doc Watson, Mississippi John Hurt, Blind Lemon Jefferson, Bert Jansch, Merle Travis, and John Fahey. There are of course many other fine and original players. (Many examples of the music of these and other performers have been collected by Happy Traum — published by Oak Publications — whose books are strongly recommended to those interested in pursuing this style.)

Silver Sand Rag

Frederick Noad

CHAPTER FOURTEEN

CLASSICAL SOLO PLAYING

Previous chapters of this book have served to introduce the reading and playing of music for guitar on a general basis. In the last two chapters in particular material was presented mostly with a view to accompanying the voice. Many people, however, after they have gained some experience, prefer to specialize in solo playing. For this reason the following two chapters will deal with the two major fields of solo performance respectively: classical and flamenco.

The word "classical" may be somewhat misleading since it is used to convey the whole field of non-folk music composed for the guitar, whether Classical, Romantic, or Modern. It also includes transcriptions of music originally written for the lute, harpsichord, or other instruments but adapted for guitar to enrich the literature available to the soloist. Classical playing requires constant practice and careful attention to the rules of technique, and those intending to pursue this field are advised to continue their studies on the following lines.

How to Practice

The results of practice depend on two things: the amount of time allotted to working, and the way in which that time is used. Many hours may be spent on essentially useless exercises or on the repetition of pieces already thoroughly practiced. The important thing is to decide how much time you wish to give to the instrument each day, and to divide that time so as to achieve maximum progress. It is a fact that one hour given to practice every day is far more valuable than two or three hours with breaks of a day or two in between. Naturally, two hours are better than one; but the amateur is normally limited in this respect, and in his case regularity is the thing to aim for above all.

Dividing Your Time

Most musicians start their practice with technical exercises to loosen the fingers and reinforce the habitual patterns of good technique. They begin by playing very slowly and positively, with great attention to detail. There is no greater fallacy than to suppose that speed is achieved by ultrarapid practice, since in nine cases out of ten this results in endless repetition of an untidy and inaccurate rendering. A passage can be played fast when it is thoroughly mastered in detail, not before then.

One of the best ways to begin your practice is the careful study of the diatonic major and minor scales. The scales exercise both hands, and are an excellent vehicle for practicing smooth position changes, accurate hand positions, and variety of tone production.

After the scales have been well practiced, time can profitably be given to arpeggios, bar exercises, ascending and descending *ligados*, and so on; but no one of these exercises will be a substitute for, or as valuable as, the diatonic scales.

After a period of technique practice, some time should always be given to sight-reading. This ability can be enormously improved by daily repetition, and should be maintained at all times. It is hard to overemphasize the importance of attaining at least reasonably good reading ability, since without this you will be limited to such few pieces as those you have memorized, and will soon bore both yourself and your listeners by your inability to broaden your musical scope. In addition, you thus rob yourself of the very considerable pleasure of running through new pieces that you have not heard before in a sufficiently fluent way to hear and enjoy them and assess their value for future memorization.

After some sight-reading it is probably best to start on those repertoire pieces you are preparing, emphasizing those that you know least well. The detailed and careful work necessary to prepare and memorize a piece should be approached analytically, and difficult passages repeated slowly and with the greatest regard for accuracy. If some small phrase or passage seems constantly to elude you it will sometimes be of assistance to write it out. This often helps the memory and unravels the difficulty.

Finally the last part of your daily practice is reached, which so many amateurs unfortunately make the first: the playing of repertoire pieces you have already learned well so as to retain them in your memory, polish them, and of course enjoy the sheer pleasure of performing them. This is usually the most enjoyable part of practice for most people, which is why so many start their practice sessions this way. But what in this case happens is that the extra determination and discipline necessary for the other phases tend to evaporate, and in fact very little is achieved.

Attention to Melody

When the guitar is used to accompany the voice, its role is largely subsidiary and harmonic, as opposed to melodic. In solo music, however, it is necessary for the guitarist to bring out both melody and harmony in the correct balance, and in view of the "smaller voice" of the guitar it is often necessary to emphasize the melodic line while subduing the accompaniment. The most usual method of achieving this is by using the rest stroke where possible for the melody, with lighter free strokes for the accompaniment.

Consider this passage from a study by Fernando Sor; play it through first as a series of simple arpeggios; then play it again using rest strokes on the accented notes, and notice how the melody emerges and the passage comes to life.

Tone Production

The quality and contrast of tone that can be produced on the guitar are almost infinite in variety, and in the long run it is the individual taste and inventiveness of the player that determines their use. Broadly speaking, the main contrasts are achieved as follows.

For a thin, clear, harpsichord-like tone use the RH near the bridge. This is more marked when playing any string open in the first position and the 1st string in all positions, and may be still further emphasized by using free strokes sharply plucked with the RH fingernails.

For a very sweet, mellow tone the RH plays near the soundhole, and where possible the melody is placed on the higher positions of the 2nd or 3rd strings instead of the 1st. In these positions vibrato is effective, and great sensitivity and delicacy may be achieved.

Between these extremes lie infinite grades of tone, and the greatest pleasure can be found in experimenting with them and applying them correctly and tastefully to pieces in preparation.

As study and recreation before continuing to the study of flamenco, try the arrangement of "Greensleeves" that follows.

Greensleeves

English Traditional
Arr. Frederick Noad

This very beautiful centuries-old melody—of unknown origin, although sometimes attributed to Henry VIII—is one of the most popular ever written.

You should play the first part at moderate speed, rippling the chords and bringing out the melody with rest strokes. Variation I may be used to practice the tremolo, which should flow smoothly and evenly. In Variation II use rest strokes to bring out the upper part, particularly the half notes that begin the measures.

Variation I

Greensleeves cont.

Variation II

CHAPTER FIFTEEN

PLAYING FLAMENCO MUSIC

Many people have only the vaguest idea of what flamenco music is, and indeed its origins are still somewhat cloudy; but the would-be interpreter of this style should have at the outset a clear idea of the historic role of the guitar in flamenco, as the instrument is essential to any sort of performance.

Although it is customary now to hear it solo on records and even in the concert hall, the flamenco guitar is by tradition essentially an accompanying instrument. Its birth was in Andalusia, a province of southern Spain that still bears many signs of the Moorish occupation and includes a highly individualistic gypsy minority. Its emergence was probably toward the end of the eighteenth century, coinciding with the growth of *cante flamenco* ("flamenco song"), with which it is closely associated and from which its inspiration is derived. The role of the guitar in accompanying the flamenco singer was far more extensive than in other types of singing at the time. Not only did it provide the rhythmic and harmonic pattern for the song, but it used evocative improvisation and subtle suggestion, emphasis, and sympathy to create an emotional mood in both singer and audience conveying all the song's intensity and passion.

The songs of flamenco express the poetry and emotions of life, often with a moral and always with something definite to say. From this very personal and deeply felt form of expression arose the varied patterns and phrases of flamenco guitar.

The guitar music itself was made up of two distinct parts: *rasgueo*, or strumming, to give a distinct harmony and rhythm to each of the song forms; and the *falseta*, an essentially melodic, short phrase used between verses of the song to sustain and add to the mood suggested by the singer.

To this day, flamenco music is made up of *rasgueo* and *falseta*. When the guitar is used to accompany dancers, the percussive *rasgueo* and *golpe* set a firm rhythmic pattern, and only a few *falsetas* are heard, usually simple ones. In solo performance, however, the *falseta* is predominant; the pieces are created by the individual player by selecting and arranging *falsetas* in a coherent sequence. These *falsetas* may be drawn from the wealth of improvisation of past players or be the creation of the current player; usually they come from both sources.

How to Approach Flamenco

Flamenco music is traditionally passed from father to son or player to player; because of this—and because of the difficulty of writing the *rasgueo* in music notation—few pieces are published, and those that are published are often incomplete. The learner in Spain has ample opportunity to hear and copy the technique of good performers, but abroad this is often impossible. Fortunately, the wide availability of flamenco recordings nowadays helps to solve this problem, since excellent players may be listened to critically and repeatedly in the home; indeed this is the best and most fruitful form of study in the absence of a teacher. At first the music may seem without logical coherence, but as the forms are studied one by one it becomes possible to see the patterns and compare the approaches of different players.

It is a good idea to study the aspects of flamenco one at a time, learning first the characteristic *rasgueo* which sets the rhythmic and harmonic pattern. When this is clearly in mind, *falsetas* may be collected from such written music as is available or from records. These *falsetas* can then be arranged in a sequence to form a coherent piece.

Flamenco Position

The technique involved in playing flamenco guitar is not greatly different from general guitar technique. The rules for the LH are identical. Because of the more extensive use of the RH thumb and various percussive effects, however, the guitar is traditionally held differently, as in Figure 33; this makes the RH technique easier to execute.

Since most flamenco is played in the first position, the changes in pitch required to accommodate different singers are accomplished by use of the *cejuela* or capotasto. Even for solos the *cejuela* is often used, normally at the 2nd fret, since the shorter distance between frets obtained somewhat facilitates the technique of the LH, and the higher pitch and greater brilliance are more typical of flamenco.

Types of Flamenco with Their Rasgueado Patterns

The general principles of the *rasgueado* have been dealt with in the section on special effects in Chapter Twelve (pp. 107ff); the student of flamenco will find that this technique needs considerable practice at first. It is most important to make the rhythmic stresses at the right points, since the ultimate rhythmic pattern is largely dependent on these; for this purpose a series of practice patterns is given below. Included in these patterns is practice for the *golpe* (p. 114 above), also an integral part of flamenco technique. Refer back to pp. 110–113 for explanations of notation used here.

Figure 33. Flamenco Position

Rhythm of Tanguillo

A word-rhythm for this is "Tiki-*pom*-tiddeley-pom, tiki-*pom*-tiddeley-pom, tiki . . ."

This example should be played using the three-finger *rasgueado*, leading with the *a* finger. Immediately after the *i* finger has completed the *rasgueado* it is pulled back for the upstroke without any pause, the complete movement making the "tiddeley-pom" rhythm.

Rhythm of Fandango de Huelva

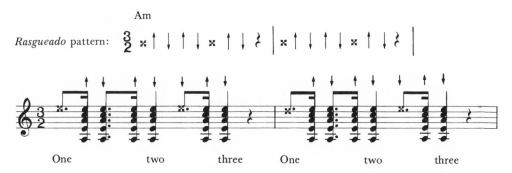

Word rhythm: "*Bump*-a-dump-a-dump, bump-a-dump; *bump*-a-dump-a-dump, bump-a-dump." ("Bump" refers to the *golpe*.)

Rhythm of Soleares

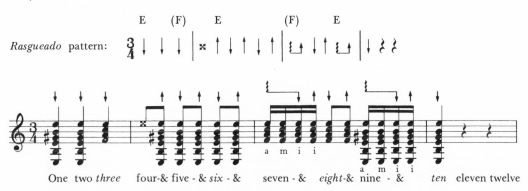

Word rhythm: "One-two-three, bump-and-two-and-*three*-and, tiddle-iddle-*om*-pom-tiddle-iddle-*pom*."

The *soleares* rhythm is built on a twelve beat form, with accents on the third, sixth, eighth, and tenth beats.

The *alegrías por rosas*, always played in E, follows a similar rhythmic pattern, and may be played by substituting a B7 chord for the F. (See p. 148 for an example of this.)

Rhythm of Siguiriyas

143

Playing Flamenco Music

Word rhythm: "Pom pom, *pom*-ti-ti *pom*-ti-ti *pom*."

This is one of the most difficult rhythms to master and should be practiced thoroughly as shown, continuing each rhythmic group into the next without any pause, since each group ends on the first beat of the bar and you continue immediately on the second beat to start the next group. The chord does not change from A major.

When you are thoroughly familiar with this, a *rasgueado* may be inserted in place of the simple strokes at the points shown.

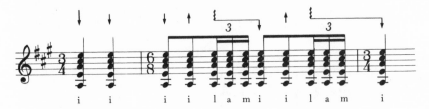

This could also be notated as follows (see *Siguiriyas*, p. 151):

Word rhythm: "Pom-pom, *pom*ty-prrr*om*pty-prrr*om*."

The *rasgueado* should roll evenly, ending with a stress as the *i* finger crosses the strings to complete it. The reason for this is that in each case the *rasgueado* is substituting for a pair of beats, a weak followed by a strong one.

Remember that nobody finds the flamenco rhythms easy at first, not even a Spaniard; but it is the unusual and unfamiliar patterns of these rhythms that make them interesting to learn.

Related Forms

The forms whose *rasgueados* you have just learned are the four basic forms of flamenco. There are many others, but most are either derived from or related to these four.

Tanguillo ("little tango"), always in the key of A, is the commonest member of the *tango* group. The gay *zapateado* ("stamping"), a fast dance used to display footwork, is essentially a *tanguillo* in the key of C. The serious and melancholy *tientos* ("prelude"), in the key of A, combines a slow version of the basic *tango* rhythm with a chord pattern similar to that of the *siguiriyas* (see below). The *farruca*, a bold, fairly fast dance in A minor, is also sometimes classed in the *tango* group, but its rhythm—a straightforward *one*-two-three-four—is considerably simpler than that of the other members of the group.

The *fandango* group is the largest of the four. The original *fandango* is an old form in which the guitar gives a simple accompaniment in the key of E in relatively free rhythm. The *fandango* was adapted and modified in different lo-

144

calities, as for instance in the region around the town of Huelva, where it became the fast, rhythmic, and very gay *fandango de Huelva* you have practiced. *Peteneras*, which combines the basic *fandango* chord pattern with a characteristic alternation of measures in ¾ and ⅜, has already appeared in this book as the piece on p. 124. From Malaga comes the familiar, lyrical *malagueñas*, also in E, not difficult technically but requiring a good deal of understanding of the feeling it conveys. Its companion piece, the *verdiales*, is more straightforward and lighthearted. The *granadinas* (from Granada, of course) is a free form in the key of B, often played as a guitar solo. Three forms from the mining community of southern Spain have a strongly Moorish flavor: *tarantas*, *mineras*, and *cartageneras*. All three are played in the unusual key of F♯, with subsidiary excursions into the chords of G and D. The bright sound of the two latter chords contrasts strongly with the darker F♯, making an interesting harmonic pattern suitable for solo improvisation.

The austere *soleares* ("song of loneliness"), in the key of E, has given rise to two very popular forms. *Bulerias* ("joking"), originally a *soleares* in the key of A, is today usually played as a very fast piece with considerable fire and verve. It is one of the most exciting forms to hear, but requires considerable technique and should not be approached without a thorough grounding in other forms. *Alegrías* ("gaiety"), also in the key of A, is perhaps the most frequently played of all flamenco forms. It is fast, vivacious, and possesses considerable charm. Occasionally it is played in the key of E, when it is conventionally called *alegrías por rosas*.

Siguiriyas (a gypsy version of the word "*seguidillas*"), from which the last group has developed, is considered the profoundest of all flamenco forms. Having the same rhythm and general form, but normally played in the key of E, is the *serranas*, the song of the *sierras* or mountains.

Lying outside the four main groups is the *sevillanas*, a gay, lighthearted folk-music form danced in a group, somewhat like a square dance. It may be played in any of several keys, and is simple enough to be suitable for the beginning guitarist.

Mastering What You Have Learned

The forms suggested for first study are the *soleares, alegrías, fandango de Huelva,* and *siguiriyas,* which are very typical and representative of the flamenco style and have the additional advantage that they may be played with simple *falsetas* yet still sound correct and expressive. The *soleares* and *siguiriyas* are melancholy and serious in their feeling, while the *alegrías* and *fandango de Huelva* express joy and optimism. Brief examples of each of these, containing *rasgueo* and *falseta*, follow.

Soleares

Arr. Frederick Noad

D. C. al Fine

Alegrías por Rosas

Arr. Frederick Noad

Fandango de Huelva

Arr. Frederick Noad

The *rasgueados* in this piece should be played using the little finger as well as the others, so as to have four sixteenth notes before pulling back with the *i* finger for the following chord.

The accompaniment to the copla fol-

lows the rhythm explained on p. **86** ; this should be practiced separately. The copla is usually sung, but is arranged here so that it may be played on a second guitar. The *x* indicates a *golpe* tap, here done with the ring finger of the right hand.

Siguiriyas

Arr. Frederick Noad

CHAPTER SIXTEEN

GOING ON FROM HERE

If you have managed to reach this point without undue difficulty you are un-doubtedly well on your way to becoming a competent player. It is difficult to estimate even aproximately how long it has probably taken you to master the contents of this book; but if the period has been less than two years you may consider your aptitude above average.

Most likely you will have found progress on the guitar to be a process of sur-mounting a series of walls, each higher than the one before; it is important to realize that this is normal in the pursuit of most arts. It is also normal to en-counter periods of frustration and apparent lack of progress, and indeed most unusual if you do not. However, in all the arts there is pleasure in pursuit as well as in achievement, and even in the greatest difficulties there is a fascina-tion.

It is important to be willing to go back over ground already covered as a means of solving difficulties. Often the trouble will be not so much the difficul-ty of the new chapter as the fact that the old one was not thoroughly mastered. Probably you have done this many times already; the main thing is to realize that this is standard procedure, not in any sense a sign of lack of ability.

Another most normal frustration is the inability to perform for other people a piece that you think you have perfected playing alone. There is a very simple reason for this. Any performance, whether for a large audience or a single friend, is a recital, and must be treated as such. The consciousness of even one listener affects the concentration and memory to a degree that varies according to the temperament of the player, and as a result an apparently well-memo-rized piece may seem to fade from the mind. The solution normally is to pre-pare the piece to a far greater degree than is necessary for playing in private, only performing it when it is so well lodged in the memory that you feel your fingers could carry on even if your mind was thinking of something completely different while playing. In nine cases out of ten, nervousness in performance is due to insufficient preparation. Also, like other aspects of guitar playing, pub-lic performance improves considerably with practice; the nervous player should take every opportunity to perform, whether at home or outside—for instance, at a local guitar society. Again, it is important to realize that nervousness in performing is by no means unusual, and should be approached like any other technical problem. As a final word on performance, remember that a simple piece well played is infinitely more pleasant to listen to than a difficult one played even slightly imperfectly; choose a program well within your capacity and avoid the temptation to air your hardest piece.

The enthusiast nowadays can find guitar societies all over the world which are only too pleased to welcome new members. In addition, there are several magazines devoted to the instrument which have regular articles on technique, the history of the guitar, and allied topics, as well as reports and reviews of concerts and recordings. Among those in the English language the following may be recommended:

THE GUITAR REVIEW   409 East 50th Street, New York N.Y. 10022
Under the editorship of Vladimir Bobri, the *Guitar Review* continues to be the leading magazine in the classical guitar field. Published three times a year, this non-profit periodical is an artistic marvel and winner of many awards. The high standard of articles and graphics makes each issue a collector's item.

GUITAR AND LUTE MAGAZINE 1229 Waimanu Street, Honolulu, Hawaii, 96814
Covering both guitar and lute, this new (since 1977) quarterly has interesting articles on technique, personalities, and worldwide happenings such as concerts, competitions, workshops, and so on.

GUITAR PLAYER   Box 615, Saratoga, California 95070
Mainly concerned with popular styles, this monthly also includes articles on the classical guitar, blues, music theory, and so on, usually by well-known performers.

THE GUITAR   20 Denmark Street, London WC2 H8NE
This monthly covers many styles, interviews, personalities, reviews new books and records, and contains much else of general interest.

It is impossible to have done complete justice to the guitar in the few pages of this book, but it is my hope that they have at least introduced you to the lure of this small instrument of such great beauty.

SONGS FOR CHORD PRACTICE

Table of Contents

On Top of Old Smokey

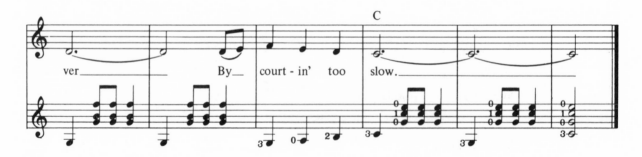

2. Now, courtin's a pleasure,
   And parting is grief;
   But a false-hearted lover,
   Is worse than a thief.

3. A thief will just rob you
   And take all you have,
   But a false-hearted lover
   Will lead you to the grave.

4. The grave will decay you
   And turn you to dust,
   There ain't one in a million
   A poor girl (boy) can trust.

5. They'll hug you and kiss you
   And tell you more lies
   Than the crossties on a railroad
   Or the stars in the skies.

When the Saints Go Marching In

2. Oh, when the new world is revealed,
   Oh, when the new world is revealed,
   Lord, how I want to be in that number,
   When the new world is revealed.

3. Oh, when they gather 'round the throne,
   Oh, when they gather 'round the throne,
   Lord, how I want to be in that number,
   When they gather 'round the throne.

Erie Canal

get to Buf - fa - lo,_____ 'til we get to Buf - fa - lo.

2. We were loaded down with barley,
   We were chuck full up of rye,
   And the captain, he looked down at me
   With his goddam wicked eye.
   Chorus

3. Our captain, he came up on deck
   With a spy glass in his hand,
   And the fog, it was so damn thick
   That he couldn't spy the land.
   Chorus

4. Our cook, she was a grand old gal,
   She had a ragged dress;
   We hoisted her upon a pole
   As a signal of distress.
   Chorus

Greensleeves

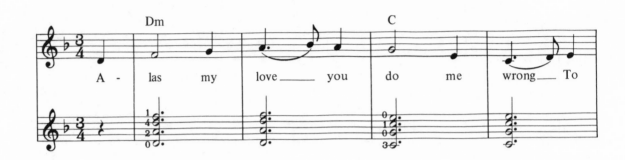

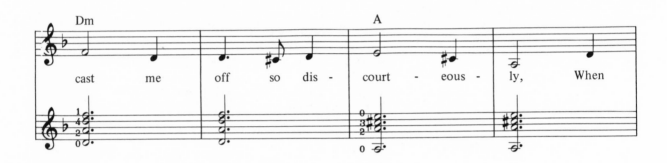

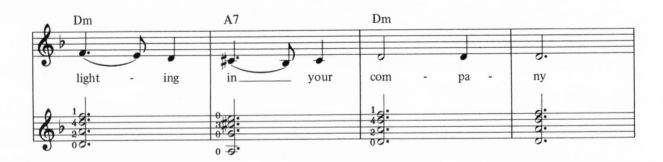

2. I have been ready at your hand,
   To grant whatever you would crave;
   I have both wagered life and land,
   Your love and goodwill for to have.
   Chorus

3. I bought you kerchiefs for your head
   That were wrought so fine and gallantly;
   I kept you both at board and bed
   Which cost my purse well favoredly.
   Chorus

4. Well, I will pray to God on high
   That you my constancy mayst see;
   And that yet once before I die,
   You will vouchsafe to love me.
   Chorus

5. Ah, Greensleeves, now farewell, adieu,
   To God I pray to prosper thee;
   For I am still thy lover true
   Come once again and love me.
   Chorus

Songs for Chord Practice

Blue-Tail Fly

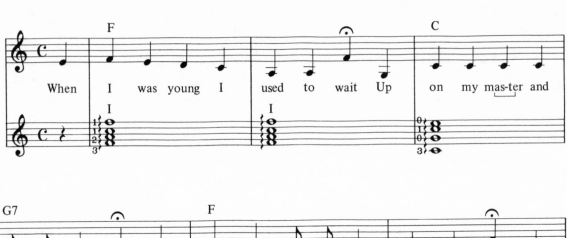

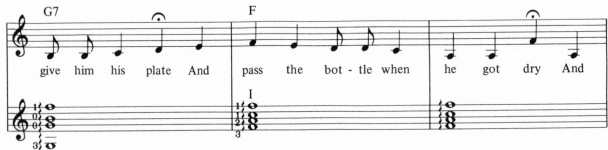

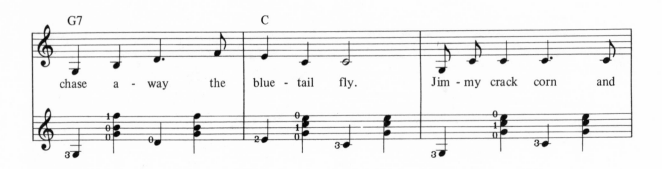

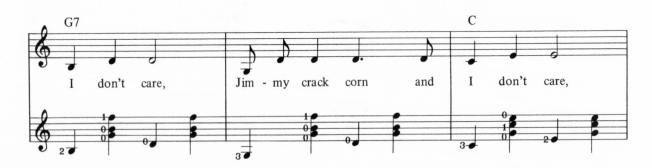

Jim - my crack corn and I don't care, My mas - ter's gone a - way.

2. And when he'd ride in the afternoon,
   I'd follow after with a hickory broom;
   The pony being rather shy
   When bitten by the blue-tail fly.
   Chorus

3. That pony run, he jump, he pitch,
   He tumble master in the ditch,
   He died and the jury wondered why;
   The verdict was the blue-tail fly.
   Chorus

4. They laid him under a 'simmon tree;
   His epitaph is there to see;
   "Beneath this stone I'm forced to lie,
   The victim of the blue-tail fly."
   Chorus

Lord Randall

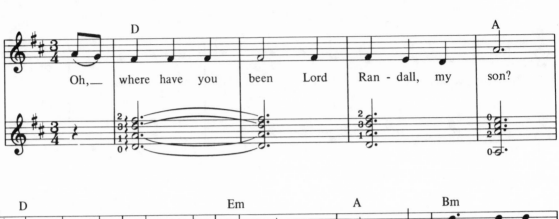

Oh,— where have you been Lord Ran-dall, my son?

Where have you been oh my pret-ty one? I've been to my

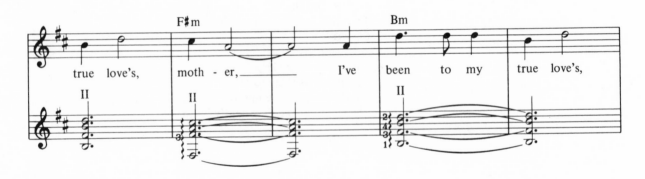

true love's, moth-er,——— I've been to my true love's,

moth-er.——— Oh— make my bed soon for I'm sick to my

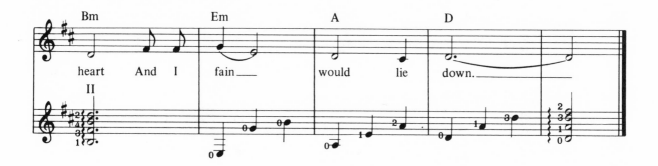

heart   And   I   fain___   would   lie   down.___

2. What did you have for your supper, my son?
   What did you have, oh my pretty one?
   A cup of cold poison, mother,
   A cup of cold poison, mother.
   Oh, make my bed soon, for I'm sick to my heart
   And I fain would lie down.

3. Oh, what will you leave your father, my son?
   Oh, what will you leave him, my pretty young one?
   My wagon and oxen, mother,
   My wagon and oxen, mother.
   Oh, make my bed soon, for I'm sick to my heart
   And I fain would lie down.

4. Oh, what will you leave your mother, my son?
   What will you leave me, my pretty young one?
   My house and my lands, mother,
   My house and my lands, mother.
   Oh, make my bed soon, for I'm sick to my heart
   And I fain would lie down.

5. Oh, what will you leave your true love, my son?
   What will you leave her, my pretty young one?
   A rope to hang her, mother,
   A rope to hang her, mother.
   Oh, make my bed soon, for I'm sick to my heart
   And I fain would lie down.

Streets of Laredo

2. "I see by your outfit that you are a cowboy"—
   These words he did say as I boldly stepped by—
   "Come sit down beside me and hear my sad story;
   I was shot in the breast and I know I must die."

3. "'Twas once in the saddle I used to go dashing,
   It was once in the saddle I used to go gay;
   First to the dram house and then to the cardhouse;
   Got shot in the breast and I'm dying today."

4. "Get six jolly cowboys to carry my coffin;
   Get six pretty maidens to carry my pall;
   Put bunches of roses all over my coffin,
   Roses to deaden the clods as they fall."

5. "Oh, beat the drum slowly and play the fife lowly,
   And play the dead march as you carry me along;
   Take me to the green valley and lay the sod o'er me,
   For I'm a young cowboy and I know I've done wrong."

Poor Boy

2. I followed her for months and months,
   She offered me her hand;
   We were just about to be married, when
   She ran off with a gambling man.
   Chorus

3. He came at me with a big jackknife,
   I went for him with lead,
   And when the fight was over, poor boy,
   He lay down beside me, dead.
   Chorus

4. They took me to the big jailhouse;
   The months and months rolled by;
   The jury found me guilty, poor boy,
   The judge said, "You must die."
   Chorus

5. And yet they call this justice, poor boy,
   Then justice let it be!
   I only killed a man that was
   A-fixing to kill me.
   Chorus

I Know Where I'm Going

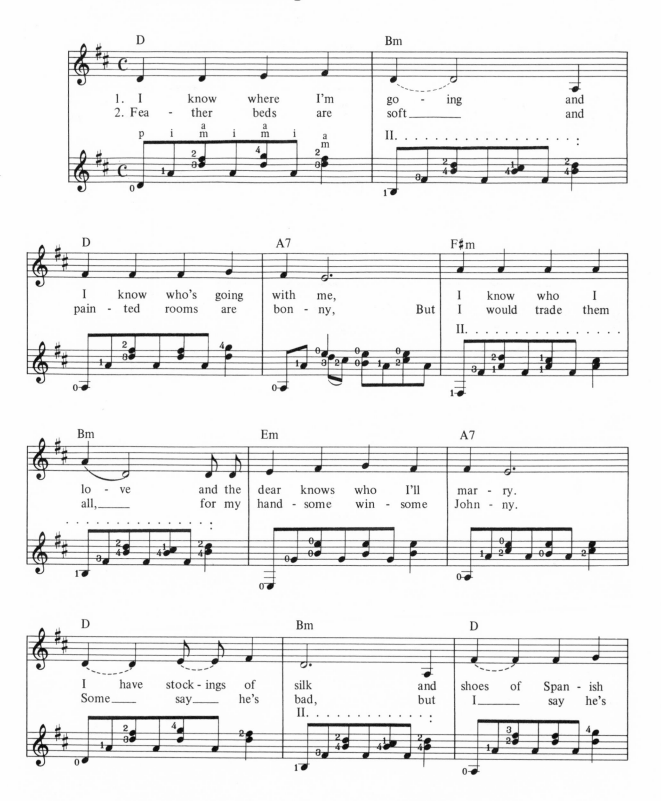

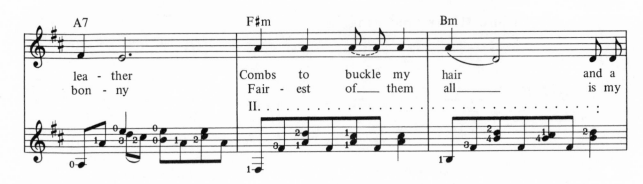

lea - ther
bon - ny

Combs to buckle my hair
Fair - est of___ them all_____

Bm
and a
is my

II. . . . . :

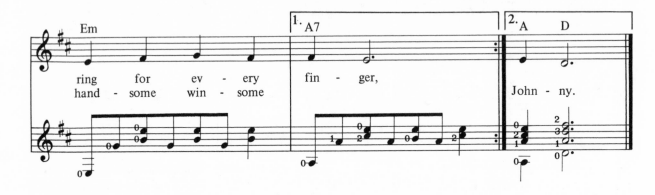

Em
ring for ev - ery
hand - some win - some

1. A7
fin - ger,

2. A D
John - ny.

170

Coplas

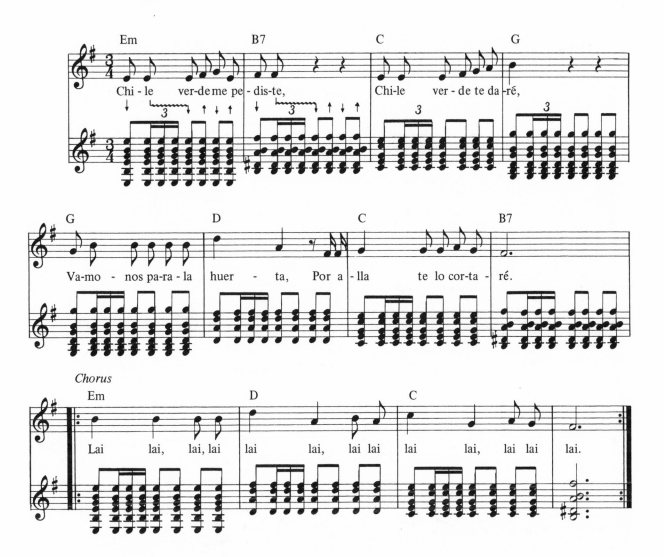

2. Dicen que los de tu casa,
   Ninguno me puede ver,
   Diles que no batan l'agua,
   Que al cabo lo han de beber,

3. La mula que yo monté,
   La monta hoy mi compadre,
   Eso a mi no me importa,
   Pues yo la monté primero.

4. La noche que me casé,
   No pude dormirme un rato,
   Por estar toda la noche,
   Corriendo detras de un gato.

5. Me dijiste fué un gato,
   El que entro por tu balcón,
   Yo no he visto gato prieto,
   Con sombrero y pantalón.

Come All You Fair and Tender Ladies

2. I wish I were some little sparrow
   And I had wings with which to fly.
   I'd fly away to my false lover
   And when he'd speak I would surely cry.

3. "Don't you recall our courting days,
   When your head lay upon my breast.
   You made me believe by the dying stars
   That the sun rose in the west!"

4. But I am not a little sparrow;
   I have no wings nor can I fly.
   I will lay me down to weep in sorrow
   I will lay me down until I die.

Drink to Me Only With Thine Eyes

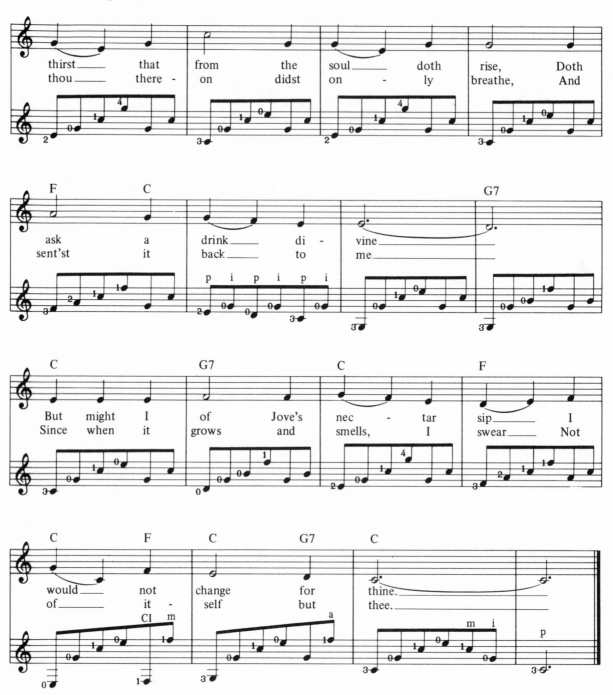

Careless Love

2. When I wore my apron low,
   When I wore my apron low,
   When I wore my apron low,
   You promised me you'd never go.

3. Now I wear my apron high,
   Now I wear my apron high,
   Now I wear my apron high,
   You pass my door and go right by.

4. I love my mom and daddy too,
   I love my mom and daddy too,
   I love my mom and daddy too,
   But I'd leave them both to go with you.

Banks of the Ohio

I asked my love to go with me,
To take a walk a lit - tle walk;
And as we walked and as we talked
A - bout our gol - - - den wed-ding day.

2. I asked your mother for you, dear,
   And she said you were too young;
   But only say that you'll be mine,
   And happiness with me you'll find.

3. I held a knife against her breast
   As gently in my arms she pressed,
   Crying, "Willie, oh Willie, don't murder me,
   I'm unprepared for eternity."

4. I started home 'twixt twelve and one,
   Crying, "My God, what have I done?
   I killed the only woman I love,
   Because she would not be my bride."

Venezuela

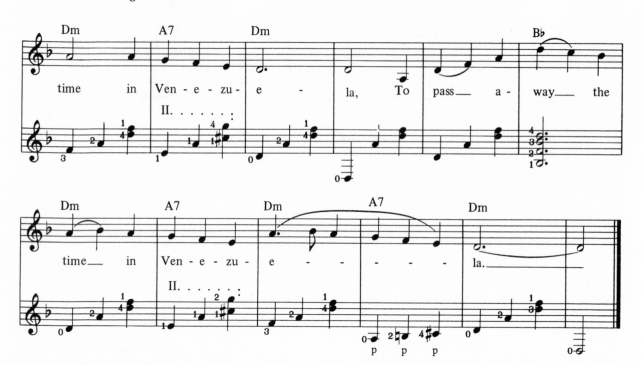

time in Ven - e - zu - e - la, To pass a - way the

time in Ven - e - zu - e - - - - la.

2. I bought her a beautiful sash of blue,
   A beautiful sash of blue,
   Because I knew what she would do,
   With all the tricks I knew she knew,
   To pass away the time in Venezuela,
   To pass away the time in Venezuela.

3. And then the wind was out to sea,
   The wind was out to sea,
   And she was taking leave of me,
   I said, "Cheer up there'll always be,
   Sailors on leave ashore in Venezuela,
   Sailors on leave ashore in Venezuela."

Blow the Candles Out

2. I like your well behavior
And thus I often say,
I cannot rest contented
Whilst you are far away.

The roads they are so muddy,
We cannot get about,
So roll me in your arms, love,
And blow the candles out.

Henry Martin

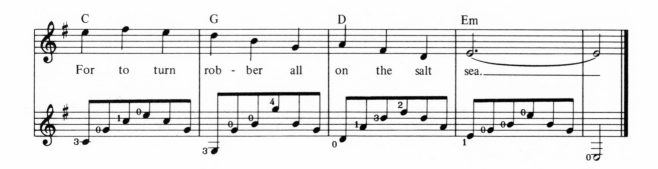

For to turn rob - ber all on the salt sea.

2. The lot it fell upon Henry Martin
   The youngest of all the three,
   That he should turn robber all on the
   Salt sea, salt sea, salt sea,
   For to maintain his two brothers and he.

3. He had not been sailing but a long winter's night,
   And part of a short winter's day,
   When he espied a lofty stout ship,
   Stout ship, stout ship,
   Come a-running down him straightway.

4. "Hello, hello," cried Henry Martin,
   "What makes you sail so high?"
   "I'm a rich merchant ship bound for fair London town,
   London town, London town.
   Will you please for to let me pass by?"

5. "Oh no, oh no," cried Henry Martin,
   "That thing it can never be,
   For I have turned robber all on the salt sea,
   Salt sea, salt sea,
   For to maintain my two brothers and me.

6. "So lower your topsail and brazen up your mizzen,
   Bow yourself under my lee,
   Or I shall give you a fast flowing ball,
   Flowing ball, flowing ball.
   And your dear bodies shall drown in the sea."

7. The rich merchant vessel was wounded full score,
   Straight to the bottom went she,
   And Henry Martin sailed off on the salt sea,
   Salt sea, salt sea,
   For to maintain his two brothers and he.

8. Bad news, bad news to old London came,
   Bad news to fair London town,
   There was a rich vessel and she's cast away,
   Cast away, cast away,
   And all of her merry men drowned.

House of the Rising Sun

2. Now if I had a-listened to what my mama said,
   I'd have been at home today,
   But being so young and foolish, oh Lord,
   I let a ramblin' man lead me astray.

3. Go tell my baby sister,
   Don't do what I have done,
   Please shun that house in New Orleans
   They call the Rising Sun.

4. Lord, I'm going back to New Orleans
   My race is almost run;
   Yes, I'm going back to spend my life
   Beneath that Rising Sun.

FORMATION OF COMPLEX CHORDS

Since it is as a practical matter impossible to show all chords in chart form, the following guide is given to show you how to make chords yourself, following simple rules.

Just as a major chord becomes a dominant seventh by the addition of an extra note, so other chords are changed in flavor by the addition of particular notes that give them a new characteristic. This is best considered in conjunction with the major scale.

The *tonic* (major) chord is formed from the 1st, 3rd, and 5th notes of the major scale; the *subdominant* (minor) from the 4th, 6th, and 8th; the *dominant* (major) from the 5th, 7th, and 2nd; and the *relative minor* from the 6th, 1st, and 3rd.

The dominant seventh is formed by adding to the dominant the seventh note above the dominant root. In this case, counting up seven notes from G we reach F, the note which makes the dominant seventh.

Other chords are formed as follows:

For the sixth chord, add the 6th note of the scale to the tonic chord.

For the ninth, add the 9th note above the root to the dominant seventh.

183

For the minor seventh, add the 7th note above the minor root to the minor chord.

Am7

For the major seventh, raise the 7th note of the dominant seventh by a semitone.

Gmaj7

Diminished Chords

Diminished chords are easy to form, since they are built of four notes evenly separated by a minor third (a tone and a semitone, or three frets on the guitar).

└1½┘ └1½┘ └1½┘   C dim.

In view of this pattern only three distinct diminished chords exist, since all others share the same notes.

Transferring the Chords to the Guitar

The above theoretical examples of chords are not always suitable for the guitar in their basic form. This shows you the notes of which the chord should consist, but which octave they should be played in on guitar depends on convenience of fingering and the musical requirements of the particular piece. For instance, having established that a C major chord is made from C, E, and G, a convenient distribution on the guitar would be this:

Although here the octave and sequence have been changed, the C remains at the base of the chord. If a chord is formed based on one of the other notes it is known as an *inversion*, and has a different characteristic sound.

Which Notes to Double

When full chords are required, some notes must recur—that is, be doubled—in another octave. As a general rule, the 1st and 5th of the scale may be freely doubled, but not the 3rd. At other times you may want to omit a chord note: The 5th may often be omitted without destroying the characteristic of the chord, but the 3rd is necessary to establish the major or minor mode.

There are many rules, and those who wish to pursue the subject will find textbooks on harmony readily available in most bookshops. There is, however, also great benefit to be derived from practical experimentation, both for memorizing chords and for training the ear.

ADDITIONAL STUDY MATERIAL

The author has written a number of works directed to further development in different areas. Their particular purposes and characteristics are as follows:

SOLO GUITAR PLAYING (2 vols.) Schirmer Books, 866 Third Avenue, New York, N.Y. 10022

This is a graded course in classical guitar performance. The higher positions are introduced in a logical progression, together with a considerable repertoire of pieces. Book Two specializes in the styles of different periods and deals with advanced technique.

THE GUITAR SONGBOOK Schirmer Books

This collection contains some of my favorite folk and art songs. It has easy-to-intermediate accompaniments, with chord indications for those who prefer to create their own.

THE RENAISSANCE GUITAR Ariel Music Publications, 33 West 60th Street, New York, N.Y. 10023

This anthology is for those who like the flavor of early music. Beginning with extremely simple pieces, the book explores the repertoire of the lute and early forms of the guitar. Each piece has study notes to assist in the learning process.

THE BAROQUE GUITAR Ariel Music Publications

In the same format as the above, this material covers the period 1620–1750 with selections from the literature for Baroque lute and guitar. The range is from very easy to moderately difficult.

THE CLASSICAL GUITAR Ariel Music Publications

This volume brings the series begun with *Remaissance Guitar* through the great Classical period of Sor, Giuliani, Aguado, and many others. The first part of the book has much study material by the nineteenth century guitar masters; the range is from very easy to advanced.